Matthew of Vendôme

The Art of Versification

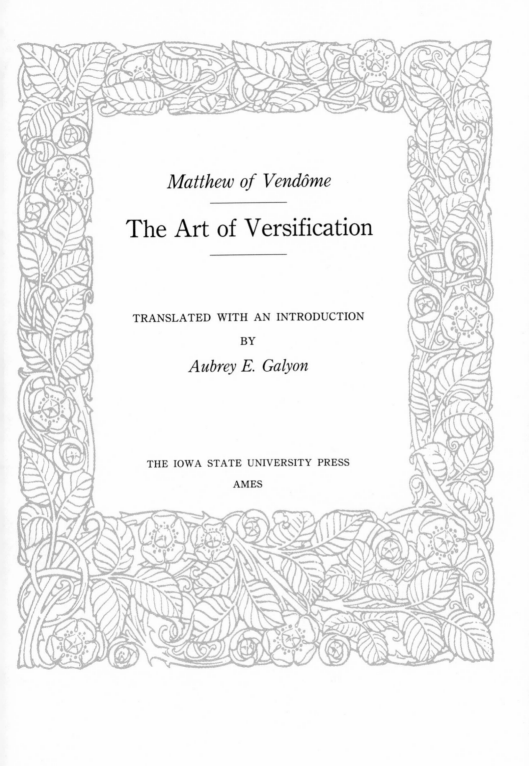

Matthew of Vendôme

The Art of Versification

TRANSLATED WITH AN INTRODUCTION

BY

Aubrey E. Galyon

THE IOWA STATE UNIVERSITY PRESS

AMES

AUBREY E. GALYON is Professor, Department of English, Iowa State University.

© 1980 The Iowa State University Press. All rights reserved

Composed and printed by The Iowa State University Press, Ames, Iowa 50010

First edition, 1980

Library of Congress Cataloging in Publication Data

Matthaeus Vindocinensis.
    The art of versification.

    Translation of Ars versificatoria.
    Includes bibliographical references and index.
    1. Poetics—Early works to 1800. I. Galyon, Aubrey, 1928–   II. Title.
PN1040.M3513   808.1   79–28313
ISBN 0–8138–1370–0

CONTENTS

P R E F A C E

This translation is based upon the text of the *Ars versificatoria* printed in Edmond Faral, *Les Arts poétiques du XIIe et du XIIIe siècle* (Paris, 1924; repr. 1962), pp. 109–93. I have followed Faral's system of numbering the sections of the *Art* and have tried insofar as possible to make the line numbers of my translations of verse passages correspond to the lineation of the Faral text.

This work was aided by a summer research grant from Iowa State University in 1976 which allowed me to pursue my study of medieval poetic theory. The staff of the Iowa State University Press, particularly Nancy Bohlen, was most helpful in the production of this book. I gratefully acknowledge my indebtedness to Professor John C. McGalliard of the University of Iowa, who read a version of this work as a Ph.D. dissertation; to Professor Valerie M. Lagorio of the University of Iowa for many valuable suggestions; and to Professor James Ruebel of the Department of Foreign Languages, Iowa State University, for his help with some of the difficult and obscure passages in Matthew's Latin. My greatest debt is to my wife and colleague Professor Linda R. Galyon whose patience, unflagging good humor, and scholarship contributed immeasurably to the completion of this book.

ABBREVIATIONS FOR TEXT CITATIONS

Internal cross references to this work are made by part number, reference number, and sometimes line number. The following abbreviations for citations are used in the Introduction and the text.

Avianus
  Fables: Fab.
Bernard of Chartres
  Cosm.: Cosmography
Cato
  Dist.: Distichs
Cicero: Cic.
  De inventione
Claudian: Claud. (These works are cited by the numbers in Gesner's edition; titles are given in square brackets following the citation.)
  Eutr.: Against Eutropius I
  Honor.: On the Fourth Consulship of Honorius
  Rufin.: Against Rufinus I
Corinthians: Cor.
Eberhard
  Lab.: Laborintus
Ennius
  Ann.: Annales
Geoffrey of Vinsauf: Geoff.
  Doc.: Documentum
Horace: Hor.
  Ep.: Epistles
  Od.: Odes
  Poet.: Art of Poetry
  Sat.: Satires
Isidore of Seville: Is.
  Etym.: Etymologies
John of Garland
  Poet.: Poetria
Juvenal: Juv.
  Sat.: Satires

Lucan: Luc.
  Phars.: Pharsalia
Martial: Mart.
  Ep.: Epigrams
Gospel of Saint Matthew: Matth.
Matthew of Vendôme: Matt.
  Milo
  Pyr. and Th.: Pyramus and Thisbe
  Tob.: Tobias
Maximian: Max
  Eleg.: Elegies
Ovid
  Am.: Amores
  Ars: Art of Love
  Her.: Heroides
  Met.: Metamorphoses
  Pont.: Pontine Letters
  Rem.: Remedy for Love
  Tr.: Tristia
Proverbs: Prov.
Prudentius
  Psych.: Psychomachia
Psalms: Ps.
Statius: Stat.
  Ach.: Achilleid
  Theb.: Thebaid
Terence: Ter.
  And.: Andria
Virgil: Virg.
  Aen.: Aeneid
  Ecl.: Eclogues (Bucolics)
  Georg.: Georgics

INTRODUCTION

The writer of verse in the Middle Ages had many authorities to consult for guidance. There were the works of classical authors, chiefly the *Ars Poetica* of Horace, the *De inventione* of Cicero, and the pseudo-Ciceronian *Rhetorica ad Herennium.*[1] From Horace one would get not only his teachings on the unity of style and concept, the harmony of the parts of a poem, and the need for careful craftsmanship but also the view that the purpose of a poem is to instruct and delight. From Cicero one would learn about *inventio* (the discovery of materials for a composition), *dispositio* (the organization of the material), and *elocutio* (putting the material into words). In addition to instruction about *inventio* and *dispositio* in the *De inventione* and *Ad Herennium,* one would find as part of *elocutio* a systematic treatment of the methods of ornamentation as means of amplification. The *Ad Herennium,* for example, lists thirty-five "figures of diction," ten tropes, and nineteen "figures of thought"; and many of these are further subdivided.

There were the encyclopedists such as Martianus Capella, Cassiodorus, and Isidore of Seville who summarized and helped spread the teachings of Cicero and the *Ad Herennium.*[2] There were also the works of grammarians such as Donatus, Priscian, Probus, and Servius.[3] The role of grammar was considerable broader than it is today. The grammarians were the main teachers of metrics and prosody as well as a major factor in the development of the system of figures and tropes. In matters of detail there was less overlapping of the classical authors and the grammarians than might appear. Of the seventeen figures of speech that Donatus discussed, fourteen were different from those in the *Ad Herennium* whose ten tropes were almost tripled in Donatus's list of twenty-eight.

There were numerous manuals, ranging from such relatively early works as Bede's *De schematibus et tropis* to the various *artes—ars dictaminis, ars praedicandi,* and *ars grammatica*—which emerged as rather late developments and continued until the close of the period.[4] The *ars praedicandi* (handbook for sermon writing), which indicated the parts of a sermon and stressed methods of amplification, was less important for medieval poetics than the *ars dictaminis* (handbook for letter

[3]

writing), which first appeared in the eleventh century. Basically
Ciceronian in orientation, these *artes* dealt with both prose and poetry;
those concerning poetry were further divided into treatments of
rhythmical composition and metrical composition, a division seen in
Thomas of Capua's *Ars dictandi* where he noted three types of writing:
prose as in Cassiodorus, metrical verse as in Virgil, and rhythmical
verse as in Primas.[5] There were *ars metrica* and *ars rithmica.*
Rhythmical verse was accentual or qualitative verse, that is, based
upon stress patterns; it was at first the verse of popular songs and only
later "won recognition as valid poetry in the hymns."[6] The verse of
classical poetry was quantitative verse, that is, based upon the quantity
or length of the syllable; such verse came to be known as metrical
verse in contrast to the newer rhythmical verse. Metrical verse was
that of the schools. Later, lists of rhetorical colors such as the *De ornamentis verborum* of Marbod of Rennes or the *Summa de coloribus
rhetoricis* of Geoffrey of Vinsauf appeared.[7]

The half-century whose midpoint is the year 1200 is marked by the
appearance of manuals of a new sort for metrical verse, the *ars poetica*
or *poetria*—treatises that discuss poetic theory as well as being guides
for the writing of Latin poetry. These arts of poetry are self-conscious-
ly theoretical works on poetics as distinct from handbooks of rhetoric,
grammar, or the *ars dictaminis.* These works have been brought
together in Edmond Faral's *Les Arts poétiques du XIIe du XIIIe siècle*[8].
The most important texts in Faral's edition are Geoffrey of Vinsauf's
Poetria nova, a work of some two thousand hexameters; his prose
treatise *Documentum de modo et arte dictandi et versificandi;* and
Matthew of Vendôme's *Ars versificatoria.*

The earliest of these is Matthew's *Art of Versification,* which was
written about 1175. The *Art* is a textbook designed to further the
writing of descriptive Latin poetry. Matthew taught at Orléans where
the work was composed, and it was most probably used there as a text
in his classes.[9] The work has four parts. The first deals with the
writing of descriptions, the second concerns elegance of diction, and
the third covers figures and tropes. The final part is a discussion of the
execution of the material and the correction of student work.

Matthew's purpose is to explain what he calls the threefold
elegance of verse. Elegy appears in a dream-vision and teaches him the
threefold system: "polished words (*verba polita*), figurative expression
(*dicendi color*), and the inner sentiment of the work (*interior favus*)" (II,
9). Part II concerning the choice of words is clearly his treatment of
polished words, and Part III on figures and tropes is his treatment of
figurative expression. Precisely where he treats the inner sentiment or
meaning is not so clear. At the beginning of Part II Matthew says that
having spoken of the writing of descriptions, he must now turn to the

threefold elegance of verse. This would seem to place what he had said about descriptions outside his tripartite scheme. Yet later he says:

> The understanding of meaning discussed above in relation to the attributes of a person or an action applies to the first member [of his threefold system, that is, meaning; his ordering of them varies]. In the example of adjectives listed according to their different endings, the second member, the elegance of words, is clearly explained; the third member, the quality of the expression, is described in the discussion of figures and tropes. (III, 51)

The discussion of descriptions in Part I is Matthew's treatment of the ideas of a poem despite the organization of his treatise which might suggest otherwise. Faral interprets *interior favus* to be "le contenu de la pensée" and says, "C'est le contenu de la pensée qui a fait le sujet du livre I."[10] This reading of Matthew is shared by Max Manitius, who writes

> Beim Beginn des zweiten Abschnitts erzählt Matthäus von einen Traume, in dem ihm die Elegie den dreifachen Reiz der Dichtkunst geoffenbart habe: über den Gedankeninhalt habe er im 1. Abschnitt gesprochen, die Form der Worte werde er im zweiten behandeln, im dritten die Wahl des Ausdrucks.[11]

The objections of Brinkmann and Kelly notwithstanding,[12] such an interpretation of Matthew's intent in the *Art* seems to be the most probable and is borne out by the fact that Matthew's interest is exclusively with descriptive poetry and by one of his definitions of verse, "the elegant combination of the words, the vivid presentation of relevant qualities, and the carefully noted epithets of each single thing" (I, 1), in which epithets, the basis of descriptions for him, are central to poetry.

Matthew concludes his instruction on writing descriptions, moreover, with this mnemonic verse:

> Who, what, where, with what aid, why, when, in what manner. (I, 116)

His attributes—status, age, occupation, sex, nationality, and so forth—are sources of material, the bases upon which students may write descriptions. The discussion of attributes is clearly his instruction about how to discover material for writing descriptions and how to use this material in a poem. Part I corresponds to *inventio* of classical rhetoric, Parts II and III to *elocutio*, and much of Part IV to *dispositio*. Matthew says that he wrote the *Art of Versification* in two months (IV, 51, 32); perhaps the confusing statements about organization of the work are the results of hasty, unrevised composition.

In the first part of this work Matthew develops an elaborate theory

of descriptions based upon attributes or epithets (the terms are interchangeable for him) and illustrates his principles with a number of
model descriptions. He lists and explains eleven personal attributes,
derived from Cicero (*De inventione* I, 24–25), and seven attributes of an
action. Since the writing of descriptions for Matthew is primarily a
matter of assigning the proper attributes to a person or an action, his
instruction consists of explaining the various attributes or giving principles for assigning attributes.

The theory of descriptions is based in part on the idea that they
should be of general types and drawn from common knowledge (I, 60).
For the poet this means essentially following traditional accounts and
accepting traditional values. Matthew can thus assert that he has
followed the chief principle of poetic practice in making certain that
the description would seem the most believable; he continues, saying,
that he spoke the truth or the semblance of truth (I, 73). By linking the
most believable description with speaking the truth, Matthew is saying
that the description is believable because it employs common
knowledge, that is, tradition and commonly accepted notions of the
qualities certain types of persons should have or traditional value. The
importance of the traditional is asserted again when Matthew writes
about the execution of the material: "Following the material they
[students] do, they seek to emulate the customary handling of events,
and thus they write with propriety or with the semblance of propriety"
(IV, 1).

The idea that descriptions should be of general types based upon
traditions or traditional values forms one-half of Matthew's theoretical
foundation for the instruction he gives for assigning the proper attribute or epithet to a person or an action. The second part of the
theory is the idea that the essential purpose of description is to praise
or blame the subject of the description. Faral has pointed out the cen-
trality of this doctrine in poetic theory and its significance for medieval
literature:

> En apparence, l'idée est accesoire; elle est, en fait, d'importance
> considérable: elle explique que, dans toute la littérature du moyen
> âge, la description ne vise que très rarement à peindre objective-
> ment les personnes et les choses et qu'elle soit toujours dominée
> par une intention affective qui oscille entre la louange et la cri-
> tique.[13]

This idea that the chief function of description is to praise or blame
dominates all Matthew's instruction about the writing of it. Even when
he is talking about the way to begin the first sentence of a poem, he
says, "If one undertakes to write approvingly about the female sex, he
might begin this way. . . . Or if he writes disapprovingly, he might
begin with the same figure. . . . One begins a piece praising or blaming

a man. . . ." (I, 7–9). His first comment on his own examples of description is: "The foregoing descriptions obviously are not all of the same type. Five commend their subjects, and two disparage them" (I, 59). He defines internal description as describing "the qualities of the inner man . . . which are set forth either for praise or censure" (I, 74). The definition of the attributes of a person or an action is informed by the same understanding: "A theme or point drawn from a name is a matter of interpreting a person's name to suggest something good or bad about the person . . ." (I, 78). Matthew tells us that "a description may be based upon time if one is able to conjecture something either good or bad about the action on the basis of the suitability of the time" (I, 106).

Matthew's principles for writing descriptions are, then, relatively simple: descriptions consist in assigning the proper attributes to a person or thing. And the purpose is to praise or blame; if such a description of a person or a thing advances the writer's purpose, the description is apt. The descriptions should be of general types, not of individuals; and, finally, the material in them should be based upon common knowledge and commonly held values.

The instruction that Matthew gives for the writing of descriptions is equally simple and straightforward. Descriptions should be full and not scanty; they "should describe not only the qualities which a person has but also those qualities which differentiate that person from others" (I, 41). He comments upon his own examples of descriptions:

> If two or more verses have the same meaning, it should be understood that these were not written frivolously but were deliberately planned to avoid imputing a fault by not mentioning a virtue and also to mention all virtues necessary to offset a possible fault. (I, 72)

The bulk of his instruction, however, concerns the assigning of proper attributes. He gives two general rules: "Any person ought to be described by epithets which show the dominant traits on which most of his reputation rests" (I, 44); and

> If one is praising people, some epithets ought to be restricted to certain types of persons, some ought to be attributed to a fair number of persons, others ought to be attributed to all praise-worthy persons generally. (I, 64)

In each of these rules one sees the importance of common knowledge and commonly held values. To illustrate the first principle, Matthew cites Horace's injunction (*Poet.*, 120):

> If as a writer you depict Achilles full of honor, make him
> Impatient, quick-tempered, ruthless, fierce; make him claim
> He is subject to no law. Make him decide everything with arms.
>   (I, 44)

As a comment on his second rule, he says that "in praising a woman one should stress heavily her physical beauty. This is not the proper way to praise a man" (I, 67). Certain qualities "ought to be attributed to any man who is praised, such as that stern manliness which maintains itself in adversity as well as in prosperity" (I, 71). And to a wife one ought to attribute "rigorous strictness, avoidance of sauciness, and shunning of incontinence and lust" (I, 69).

The rest of his instruction consists either of lists explaining the eleven personal attributes and the nine attributes of an action or of Matthew's examples of description for the writer to imitate. There is almost no commentary on the types of attributes and no indication of which ones of the eighteen he lists are apposite for a certain purpose and which are not.

Matthew is the only one of the late medieval theoreticians to consider when description is to be employed as well as the type of attribute to be used. He begins his discussion of descriptions by pointing out that "in many cases a description of the person [about whom one is writing] is fitting, in many superfluous" (I, 38). He cites two examples of the fitting use of descriptions:

> If one writes about the strength of a certain person, about his steadfastness of mind, his devotion to honesty, his refusal to be servile as we have Lucan writing of the austerity of Cato, then one ought to describe the various virtues of Cato, so that when the audience has set before them the fastidiousness of Cato's habits and the special quality of his virtue, they can more easily understand what follows about the heedlessness of Caesar and Cato's concern for liberty. (I, 39)

Or if one were to write about Jupiter's falling in love with Callisto, Matthew says that the writer must set forth Callisto's beauty so that it will seem "reasonably believable that a heart as great as Jupiter's could be heated up over the charms of a mere mortal" (I, 40). He later makes the same observation "that a description based upon time or place may often be superfluous, often apt. Unless we suggest something of importance to our listeners by details of time and place which we wrap around our account, these details ought to be omitted" (I, 110).

In common with other medieval writers Matthew notes "that a twofold description of any person is possible: one external, one internal" (I, 74). The external description concerns a person's appearance, and the internal his mind, his character, and his personality. Here the technical terms of medieval rhetoric, *effictio* (portrait) and *notatio* (character) are not used; Matthew has instead substituted his own less formal ones. This part of the theory of description is treated quite briefly by Matthew, who does insist that any description of a person should include appearance (I, 75). Matthew's own practice in his eight model descriptions (I, 50–58), however, does not follow this rule; there is little or no description of the appearance of the Pope, Ulysses, Davus, Caesar, or Marcia. In the description of Beroe and Helen only slight attention is paid to internal attributes. The eleven personal attributes listed by Matthew refer, moreover, to internal rather than external description except for "nature," which is subdivided into physical and mental and is thus a rather catchall category. On the basis of his practice as well as his theory, Matthew's idea of description does not seem to be a blend of internal and external, that is, of *notatio* and *effictio*. Despite his statement of the conventional twofold description, Matthew explicitly tells us:

> Those characteristics which are attributed to the Pope, or to Caesar, or to various persons who are described should be understood, not as peculiar characteristics of these particular persons, but as characteristics that may apply to other persons of the same social status, age, rank, office, or sex. Names of specific persons are thus used to represent a general class of persons and not to indicate special qualities belonging alone to those persons who are named. (I, 60)

This fact might explain the lack of external description of Caesar or the Pope, for Matthew is trying to depict general types of virtue and not particular men whose physical description is either possible or of interest. If this same explanation holds for the absence of internal description in the portraits of Helen or Beroe, we have one indication of the difference between twelfth- and thirteenth-century poetics and that of the Renaissance poet who could write:

> For of the soule the bodie forme doth take:
> For soule is forme, and doth the bodie make.
> > (Spenser, *An Hymne in Honour of Beautie*)

In the section on polished words Matthew has two related concerns: the proper use of words to give verse elegance and the metrical strictures that elegiac composition imposes upon word choice. He organizes the presentation of his material to give practical instruction in the writing of elegiacs. The metrical demands of the pentameter placed a premium on words ending in *-alis, -osus, -atus, -uus,* and *-aris.* The adjectives whose use Matthew discusses are those having these desirable endings (II, 14). He points out that the restrictions of the pentameter make certain words unsuitable for poetry, particularly those ending in *-ativus* (II, 25). Only certain first conjugation verbs are discussed. Matthew's interest here is also metrical, for the rhythms of these verbs make them especially suited for elegiac meters. Another indication of the metrical concerns of this section is that the words discussed are almost always illustrated in lines of verse rather than just in phrases, so that the reader can see how their use furthers the elegance of verse. When only a single line, moreover, is used to illustrate a word, it is always a pentameter; for Matthew says that it is easier to write the hexameter of a distich "since the pentameter must complete the thought of the hexameter" (II, 40).

Matthew restricts his discussion of polished words mainly to adjectives and verbs, giving the most attention to adjectives and participles. He does this because it is in these words that "the elegance of language is most frequently found. . . . This is true because there are certain proprieties in the use of these words, and elegance in versification consists in a scrupulous observation of these proprieties" (II, 12). Here he is talking about more than the sounds of the words and their metrical properties. Matthew's examples, which "show how the felicitous joining of words can be most gracefully and elegantly done" (II, 14), indicate that his concern is also with usage. He discusses the meaning of words and their connotations and denotations, redundancy, repetition, and other commonly acknowledged stylistic gaucheries.

The discussion of elegant words is in many ways the least interesting and the least informative part of the *Art*. This is particularly true for an English translation of this section. Much of Matthew's concern is with the rhythms and sounds of certain words in quantitative Latin verse, something virtually impossible to capture in English. For the most part Matthew's instruction consists of lists showing how elegant words can be used in verse. There is little commentary to guide the reader. Presumably Matthew felt that the elegance of these words and their suitability for verse would be evident from his examples of their use. He dismisses unrefined expressions "bandied about by barbers and drunks" as pointless for the discussion (II, 23), but nowhere does he give examples of these interdicted words. When Matthew turns his attention to improprieties, he is both clearer and more interesting: more interesting because many of his remarks are couched in the acerb and quarrelsome language that marks much of this work (see II, 16, for example) and clearer because even in a translation his standards for judging are more easily seen, since they depend less upon the peculiar features of Latin verse than do his criteria for elegance in diction.

The third member of his threefold system is "the quality of the expression," that is, figures, tropes, and rhetorical colors. For Matthew the use of figures and tropes is essential to poetry. Making an analogy with a sculptor's shaping the material of a statue, he says that in poetry "the material—the language—is rough and awkward until it is arranged through the artful employment of some scheme or trope or rhetorical color" (III, 2). The approach in this section is again straightforward and pedagogical; he states flatly that his purpose is to

give examples so that the listeners, in turn, may make models and examples to match those he has given (III, 17). This purpose is reflected
in the lists of figures and tropes he discusses. He points out that
although seventeen figures are usually listed, he will treat "only those
[thirteen] which can be used most elegantly in the practice of versification" (III, 3). Of tropes he says, "Although there are thirteen . . . we
must consider the ones which should especially be recommended to the
verse writer" (III, 18). He discusses eight.[14] This same practical bent
can be seen in the fact that he discusses four types of metaphor at
length, since "the versifier ought to use it often, for it gives metrical
verse an especial grace" (III, 24); but he restricts himself to a discussion of only one type of metonymy, "since the first two types are
employed less frequently by authors" (III, 30).

Matthew here as elsewhere in the *Art* gives little indication of the
criteria he uses to judge what is and what is not suitable for the writer
of verses. There is no suggestion why the four figures or the six tropes
he omits from his treatment are less useful than those he includes.[15]
The treatment in this section, however, is more elaborate than in the
others, for considerable commentary is given in an effort to make clear
precisely what each figure or trope is and how it might be used in
verse. Matthew's discussion of figures and tropes shows the influence
of Isidore of Seville and Donatus.[16] His statement that seventeen
figures and thirteen tropes are usually listed derives from Donatus,
whom Matthew uses for his treatment of tropes. His definitions of
schema and *tropos* are simplifications of Isidore's definitions, for
Matthew gives only Isidore's translations of the Greek words *schema*
and *tropos* and none of his further definitions. He bases his lists of
figures upon Isidore and follows him in giving Greek names to the
figures in contrast to the more usual Latin ones. A further indication of
Matthew's adherence to Isidore can be seen in the fact that of the
thirteen references to classical authors that Matthew uses to illustrate
figures, six are found in Isidore illustrating the same figures.

In contrast to the rather full discussion of figures and tropes,
rhetorical colors receive only the most cursory treatment. Matthew
observes "someone else" has already written about rhetorical colors
and says that his treatise is not going to be a pastiche of quotations
from another (III, 45). Matthew then lists twenty-nine rhetorical colors
to show the listener "what remains to inquire into" (III, 47). His list of
colors is derived from the *Ad Herennium* (IV, 19–41). The "someone
else" is probably Marbod of Rennes, whose list of rhetorical colors in
De ornamentis verborum corresponds exactly with Matthew's.[17] If
Marbod's book was being used where Matthew taught at Orléans, this
might explain his unwillingness to quote from it, for Matthew certainly
shows no reluctance to quote from Horace and others.

The working out or execution of the material is the last area of

major concern for Matthew. Matthew's understanding of material
seems to be the content of the poem that is given to the student for ornamentation.[18] Composition in his classes must have been similar to
what went on under the tutelage of Bernard of Chartres, whose
students, John of Salisbury tells us, were given the rough material of a
narrative or other topic which they would render into a pleasing style
of embellishment and ornamentation.[19]

Matthew's students were writing descriptive verses based upon
models for imitation. Thus *dispositio* or the organization of material
was not a major problem for them.

Dispositio gets rather slight treatment in this section. Matthew, in
common with Eberhard the German, says nothing of the distinction
between natural and artificial order, which Geoffrey of Vinsauf and
John of Garland discuss as ways of beginning a work and arranging
contents.[20] Matthew and Eberhard agree in saying that the writer can
begin with either *zeugma* or *hypozeuxis*. It is clear that the distinction
between natural and artificial order refers to arrangement of the
material (that is, the subject matter) in contrast to beginning with
zeugma or with *hypozeuxis*, which refers to methods of beginning the
first sentence of a work. The impression that Matthew views the
ordering of the material as a verbal matter rather than one of design is
borne out by the fact that his section devoted to the working out of the
material begins with a discussion of word choice (IV, 1–2). But the
question is not quite this simple. Matthew also discusses proverbs as a
way of beginning a work (I, 16). Beginning a poem with a proverb im-
plies concern for more than merely a way of starting the first sentence;
the proverb must be related to the aims of the poem. Matthew gives
more than twenty examples of how to begin a work with a proverb, obviously indicating an interest in something other than a grammatical
trick for getting started with the first sentence. Indeed, Geoffrey notes
that beginning with a proverb is one way of employing artificial order
(*Poetria nova*, 125–33; *Doc.* I, 1, 10–13). When one turns to Matthew's
remarks on the conclusion of a poem, one sees that here again he has in
mind more than a mere grammatical concept of how to end a sentence.
He says that "a conclusion, as the term is used here, is an appropriate
ending of a poem that completes its overall design" (IV, 49). He then
lists an epilogue or recapitulation of ideas, a correction, a plea for indulgence, a boast, and an expression of gratitude as possible types of
conclusions (IV, 50–51).

Matthew's remarks on describing an action also show some
awareness of the problems of organization. He asserts the rather trivial
principle that "certain actions are preludes to others and certain ones
are consequences of others" (IV, 13) and exemplifies this principle
with his version of the *gradus amoris:* seeing, desire, approach, conversation, blandishments, and union. Noting that one should "copy the

steps of an action straightforwardly, so that there is no interruption of the account," Matthew criticizes Ovid's account of Jupiter's passion for Io (*Met.*, I, 588) in which "the coherence of the account is interrupted, for two steps are omitted: desire and approach" (IV, 13).

While Matthew does pay passing attention to the organization of the material, his chief interest is with lines of poetry. This is clearly seen in his discussion of correction, which he describes as "an examination of metrical verse, removing blemishes, and setting forth graceful emendations" (IV, 32). By blemishes he evidently intends matters of expression rather than composition, for he says, "The marking of faults to be avoided comes first, and the showing of graceful expression to be chosen follows" (IV, 33), and "in verses that are separate and distinct sentences the correction ought to proceed along the lines of *zeugma* or *hypozeuxis*" (IV, 34).

This same interest in verbal details rather than the overall design of the poem is seen in his directions for making changes in material that is already versified. Matthew rather cloudily speaks of "a change of both words and meanings with an equivalent sense retained" or "a change of words only and not of meanings" (IV, 20).[21] What is meant by "a change of words only and not of meanings" seems clear enough; this is purely a matter of word choice, the use of synonyms: "Hair may become tresses, waves billows, or the wind a breeze," to cite Matthew's example (IV, 24). By a "change of both words and meanings with an equivalent sense retained," he seems to be saying that the content of the material at hand is retained and the form of the expression as well as of the words is changed; that is, active constructions are made passive or circumlocutions are used (IV, 22, 23). Here Matthew not only uses meaning in a very narrow sense but also seems to understand changes in the material in an equally narrow sense.

The theory of ornamentation in the *Art of Versification* differs considerably from the treatment accorded it in other twelfth- and thirteenth-century arts of poetry both in content and in organization of material. Matthew's threefold division—the beauty of the idea, the choice of words, and the quality of speech—is peculiar to him and contrasts with the division into difficult ornamentation and facile ornamentation common to Geoffrey, Eberhard, and John of Garland.[22]

Just as Matthew does not organize his treatment into difficult and facile ornamentation, neither does he talk about all that was traditionally subsumed under these rubrics. There is nothing of substance in the *Art* covering facile ornamentation, that is, rhetorical colors and determination. As we have seen, rhetorical colors get only the most cursory treatment; and determination—of which Faral says "Indépendamment des couleurs de rhétorique, il existe pour le style simple une seconde source d'ornement, qui est la 'détermination' "[23]—is not mentioned. Determination refers to joining a noun or an adjective or a verb to other nouns, adjectives, or verbs either as modifiers ("Cato's Marcia") or as complements ("Guido sent it, Hugo carried it, Adam received it"). John of Garland explains determination (*Poet.*, p. 903) and Geoffrey gives considerable attention to it (*Poetria nova*, 1761–1841; *Doc.*, II, 3, 48–102). Matthew's treatment of figures does embrace some of the same ones that Geoffrey illustrates in his discussion of determination (*asyndeton, synecdoche, zeugma*, and *paranomasia*), but his orientation is quite different.

Nor does one find in Matthew anything comparable to the theory of amplification and abbreviation that forms a major part of the instruction of Geoffrey, who devotes 533 lines of the *Poetria nova* (203–736) to it; it also comprises Section II, 2 of his *Documentum.* The treatment is not as full in Eberhard (*Lab.*, 299–342) and John of Garland (*Poet.*, pp. 913–18). Matthew's techniques for description have certain affinities with the theory of amplification, but the focus is not at all the same. Kelly has suggested that in Matthew's remarks on expanding partial notions (IV, 23) we see the beginning of the theory of amplification that was to be fully developed by Geoffrey some thirty years later.[24] Neither is there in Matthew anything like the theory of conversions that Geoffrey treats at length (*Poetria nova*, 1588–1760; *Doc.*, II, 3, 104–31). Conversion, as the name suggests, is that instruction which teaches how one part of speech may be converted into another (*Doc.*, II, 3, 104–18): a preposition into a verb or noun, an adjective into a noun. The technique set forth in the theory of conversions resembles those recommended by Geoffrey in advice on how one is able to be copious in creating metaphors (*Doc.* II, 3, 8–22). Matthew's directions for expanding partial notions cited by Kelly as the beginning of amplification are similar to Geoffrey's precepts on *copia.*

There is another more substantive difference between Matthew and Geoffrey, Eberhard, or John that sets his work apart from theirs. In asserting the principle that the believability and vividness of a description arise from its being of a general type and being based upon common knowledge, as well as in setting forth the kinds of attributes fit for various sorts of persons, Matthew is certainly the most explicit of the late medieval theoreticians in his treatment of meaning. Geoffrey's *Poetria nova* does give examples of descriptive portraits (554–667), of *effictio* or physical description (1259–1365), and of *notatio* or character (1366–90), but makes no comment on these descriptions. In the *Documentum,* description is considered only as one means of amplification (II, 2, 3–10). John of Garland and Eberhard are virtually silent on the content of poetry. Matthew concludes his statement of the unity of the threefold system with this comment:

> In the first part the elegance of the inner meaning is treated, in the
> second the elegance of the words, and in the third the quality of

> the expression. Here not just any order can properly be assigned
> to these three members. For just as in the division referred to
> earlier, sentiments come first, words follow, and the quality of the
> expression is given as the third member; so in the exercise of the
> poetic faculty the conceptual realization of meaning comes first,
> then language, the interpreter of understanding, follows, then the
> orderly arrangement of the treatment. Thus the conception of the
> meaning comes first, next comes the working out of the language,
> then the ordering of the treatment or the disposition of the
> material. (III, 52)

Matthew, to be sure, does not give so much attention to an explicit
treatment of the content of a poem as he does to some of the formal
aspects of poetry. Matthew's theory of poetry, however, does make it
clear that remarks like "with Matthew, poetry is nothing more than a
school exercise—the *ars poetica* and the *ars dictaminis* are on a level"[25]
and "style, which is his only concern, is conceived as decoration" or
"reference to subject, thought, or composition goes no further [than a
listing of attributes]; the rest of the book is purely verbal"[26] are to be
seen as exaggerations of Matthew's lack of concern with content. The
fact noted earlier that Matthew alone gives criteria for deciding the ap-
propriateness of descriptions should moderate such judgments as
these.

Matthew, "one of the masters of the new poetics,"[27] to use
Curtius's term, clearly views his work, dependent as it is upon ancient
authors,[28] as a distinctly modern poetic. On this point one may contrast
Matthew with an older view of Geoffrey of Vinsauf. Speaking of
Horace's *Art of Poetry,* Curtius says it "was commonly called his
Poetria. So Geoffrey of Vinsauf, author of the *Poetria nova* (ca. 1210),
intends no more by his title than to say that he is putting forth a new
poetics," that is, another poetics.[29] Matthew's language in such
passages as "also the novelty of this little book ought not be ascribed to
presumption" (*Prologue,* 4) and his remarks about the ancients show
that he considers his book a different approach to poetry. Geoffrey's
most recent translator, Jane Baltzell Kopp, disagrees with Curtius's interpretation of Geoffrey's title:

> The title of his work is an implicit claim that he would supplant the
> Latin poet Horace as arbiter of poetic doctrine. Horace's *Art of
> Poetry* was known in the Middle Ages under the title *Poetria,* so
> Vinsauf's use of the title *Poetria nova* was really an assertion that
> he was presenting "new" doctrines to replace the older ones.[30]

Whatever Geoffrey may have intended by his title, a marked difference
between Matthew, the earliest of the late medieval theoreticians, and
Geoffrey can be seen in their metrical preferences: the *Poetria nova* is
composed in the older hexameters, whereas Matthew writes only

elegiacs and discusses only this newer meter. Matthew, moreover, criticizes the ancients for padding their poetry "so that their sparse material then abounding in poetic figures might swell into artificial luxuriance." Moderns are not permitted this luxury, "for new advances put an end to old practices" (IV, 5). Indeed, for Matthew the essence of poetry is language in which there is "nothing deficient and nothing redundant" (I, 1). Among the literary vices of the ancients condemned by him are pleonasms, tautology, improper usage, faulty grammar, and inexact prosody (IV, 3–10). Writers who incur his censure for errors in grammar and usage include Virgil, Statius, Terence, Lucan, and Ovid, who oddly enough is also criticized because his narrative technique "is not handled with enough artfulness" (IV, 14). Matthew's modernity is further seen by the fact that in the Prologue he defends himself against the charge that his book represents a departure from established practice.

Another aspect of the *Art of Versification* that sets it apart from other arts of poetry is its tone. Matthew's book is often personal, abusive, and obscene. The personal tone of this work is shown not only by the autobiographical facts contained in it but also by Matthew's repeated references to his detractors, especially his redheaded rival Rufus, whom he identifies as Arnulf of Saint-Evurce (IV, 47).[31] His references to Rufus, or Rufinus as Matthew sometimes calls him, perhaps playfully referring to the hero of Claudian's poem, are abusive and often quite scurrilous (see Prologue, 2–4, for example, where he attacks Rufus and his supposed red-haired mistress Thaïs). At times Matthew goes out of his way to insult Rufus, often by an indecent affront to Thaïs (see II, 38, 41–42, for example). Matthew's use of obscenity is not restricted to his attacks on Rufus. There often seems to be no reason for his coarse sexual references except his own whims (see, for example, II, 37–38). At other times his sexual allusions indicate a playfully inventive mind, even if a somewhat pedantic one. Who but a schoolmaster would use a dactyl as a symbol of the penis and testes (I, 53, 77–80)? Since Matthew says he has written his work for the instruction of boys (II, 12 and IV, 51), some critics have been puzzled by the obscene passages in his work. Typical of this attitude is Hauréau who writes:

> Il y en a qui sont d'une incroyable indécence dans le portrait d'un parasite [I, 53]. Si mauvaise opinion qu'on ait des moeurs du moyen âge, on ne s'explique pas qu'un professeur ait pu composer de tels vers et les mettre, dans un traité didactique, sous les yeux de ses écoliers. Il n'y a rien d'une obscénité pareille même dans les *Carmina burana.*[32]

One also recalls Allen's comment on the immorality of medieval students, where he specifically mentions Matthew of Vendôme among others and says, "Evil as the morals of such students were . . . the pace was set for them by their instructors: like master like man."[33] On the other hand moral and literary tastes simply change. Speaking of the curriculum author Maximian, Curtius quotes Schanz's remark that this "poet regards obscenity as the summit of his art," and continues, "the Middle Ages—always excepting the rigorists, who were in the minority—was much less prudish than the Modern Period."[34] Perhaps one should be surprised at nothing found in Matthew, who ends a description of Helen in which he is showing his pupils how to avoid verbosity with this line: "Put Hippolytus alongside her and he will become Priapus" (I, 57, 24).

From the quotations and references in the *Art* one can see that Matthew was a learned and widely read man. Sedgwick has tabulated his quotations:

> Lucan, about 40; Statius, *Thebaid,* 25, *Achilleis,* 2; Virgil, *Aeneid,* 14 or 15, *Eclogues,* 14, *Georgics,* 1; Ovid, *Metamorphoses,* 12, *Ars Amatoria,* 10, *Heroides,* 10, *Ex Ponto,* 7, *Amores,* 7, *Remedia Amoris,* 16, *Tristia,* 5; Horace, *Epistles,* i, 15, *Epistles,* ii, 2, *Ars Poetica,* innumerable, *Satires,* 1, *Odes,* 1; Juvenal, 12, Claudian, 4; Cato, 2; Bernardus Silvestris (Matthew's master), 2; Maximian, Prudentius, Ennius, Terence, Avianus, Martial, 1 each.[35]

In addition to these Matthew also quotes or shows knowledge of Boethius, Cicero, Donatus, Isidore, Marbod of Rennes, Peter Riga, Priscian, and, of course, the Bible. Few of these furnished him more than illustrative material; but we have seen that Matthew's discussion of figures and tropes is indebted to Isidore and Donatus and his treatment of rhetorical colors is influenced by Marbod's work. The most pervasive influences on Matthew are Horace and Cicero. This, however, is not surprising, for as Faral has pointed out, they were the principal medieval authorities for the writing of descriptions.[36]

Horace is quoted so often either for examples or as an authority for what Matthew says that Baldwin writes, "The use of Horace's 'Ars Poetica' is so extensive, even for the time, as to suggest that Matthew's book may have begun in his praelections [lectures] on that poem."[37] What is important, however, is what Matthew's poetic theory owes to Horace.

The Horation emphasis on the unity of the poem is reflected in Matthew's scorn at those who "turn out their ragged verses, attempting to make a unified poem out of an assortment of trifles" (Prologue, 7). He recommends that descriptions be based upon common knowledge and generally held ideas and cites Horace's lines,

> Either follow tradition or invent
> Details that agree with each other,

as authority for his view (I, 73). Matthew quotes the *Art of Poetry* in discussing the importance of paying attention to certain characteristics in describing a person (I, 42), and the general remarks on apt descriptions (I, 39–49) reflect lines 153–78 of the *Art of Poetry*. He converts Horace's theory of style into a statement on observing propriety in descriptions: "Similarly, other qualities ought to be assigned in a variety of ways to other persons, always in keeping with Horace's dictum: 'Let each style be employed only where it is fitting' " (I, 70). Matthew permits the mixing of the serious with the jocular as a pleasant defense against boredom and takes as his authority Horace's lines:

> It is not enough that a poem be beautiful;
> It must also be charming. (II, 35)

Horace had noted the pitfalls of a long poem (*Poet.*, 360) and cautioned, "Whatever you teach, be brief" (*Poet.*, 335). Horace's confession, "I strive to be brief and I become obscure" (*Poet.*, 25) was taken to emphasize the difficulty of writing both briefly and well; thus brevity, well handled, became for some a mark of stylistic excellence.[38] Matthew does not contrast *amplificatio* and *breviatio* as styles as does Geoffrey of Vinsauf among later writers; he instead follows Horace in stressing brevity as a stylistic ideal.

Much in the tone and emphasis of Matthew's work reflects Horace's *Art of Poetry*. Horace recommends a close attention to language (*Poet.*, 46–72 esp.), and one major section of the *Art of Versification* treats the matter of word choice. Matthew, moreover, quotes Horace's statement that usage should be the rule for word choice in poetry as his own guiding principle (IV, 26). Matthew's directions for material that has previously been versified as well as for the handling of fresh material bring to mind lines 119–78 of the *Art of Poetry*.

The influence of Cicero on the *Art* does not show itself in the abundance of quotations that Horatian influence does. But much of the terminology and the theory found in Section I have their roots in Cicero. Matthew says that description of a place, for example, ought to be included only when it is relevant to one's overall purpose; he cites as an example of the proper use of topographical description, Cicero's description of the beauties of Sicily in his oration against Verres, because Verres's infamous behavior stood out in contrast to the beauty of the land (I, 110). In developing an attribute from a name, Matthew follows Cicero's precept of using the etymology of the name (I, 78; *De inventione*, I, 34); he also follows Cicero in considering nature a twofold attribute: mental and physical (I, 79).

Matthew tells us that he derives from Cicero (*De inventione*, I, 24–25) his list of eleven personal attributes such as age, sex, and so forth, which form the basis of his method of description (I, 41). It is thus interesting to note that to Cicero's list of attributes Matthew joins Horace's observations on the importance of keeping in mind differentiating qualities of the person one is describing (I, 42). Here we see one instance of what Brinkmann must have meant when he wrote, "Die Theorie des Matthaeus verbindet Vorschriften Ciceros mit der Ars poetica des Horaz,"[39] for the Ciceronian tradition is forensic and oratorical in contrast to the poetic and dramatic tone of the *Art of Poetry*.

One can see in Matthew's essentially Horatian scheme of descriptions significant indications of the forensic-Ciceronian approach as an important substratum in his methodology. This forensic interest is most apparent in Matthew's discussion of the description of an action. He defines an action as "something done or spoken on the basis of which some man or some woman may, as it were, be accused of infamous behavior; that is, the person is condemned on the basis of the charge which is lodged against him" (I, 93). Among the nine attributes of an action Matthew lists "the time" and "the place" (I, 94). Curtius has pointed out how the technical terms *argumentum a tempore* (when?) and *argumentum a loco* (where?) are derived from "the topics of proof" in forensic oratory.[40]

Most of what we know about Matthew's life and his works derives from autobiographical details furnished in his poems.[41] He was born in Vendôme around 1130. His father died while Matthew was quite young, and the boy went to Tours where he was raised by his uncle Engelbaud, the Archbishop of Tours. At Tours, Matthew studied the liberal arts under the famous Bernard Silvester. After his education at Tours he moved to Orléans where he taught grammar and wrote the *Art of Versification*. Matthew tells us that he was at Orléans during the time the poet Hugh the Primate was flourishing there. From Orléans he went to Paris, where he lived ten years and probably studied logic. He died near the end of the century.

Matthew is the author of a number of works in addition to the *Art*. In one of these, the *Poetic Epistles* (a collection of model letters), he lists fifteen of his works.[42] We can identify only two of these titles today: *Milo*, an Oriental tale of 256 elegiac verses about Milo and his wife Afra with whom a king falls in love, and a poem with a classical subject, *Pyramus and Thisbe*. His verse paraphrase of the Apocryphal *Book of Tobit, Tobias*, enjoyed considerable success in his day. This poem of more than 2100 lines is dedicated to Archbishop Bartholomew of Tours and to the archbishop's brother, the Dean of St. Martin's. Each of these three works is quoted in the *Art*.

Matthew occupied a position of considerable respect and influence in the Middle Ages. By the middle of the thirteenth century Matthew had become a "curriculum author"; in his *Laborintus* Eberhard the German lists both Matthew's *Art of Versification* and his poem *Tobias* as texts to be studied by students of his day.[43] Writing slightly earlier, Gervase of Melkley places Matthew in the company of such authors as Bernard Silvester, under whom Matthew had studied; Geoffrey of Vinsauf; and Alan of Lille.[44] Radulf of Longchamp, in a gloss on the *Anticlaudianus* of Matthew's contemporary Alan, calls Matthew a man of "wide renown and great authority."[45] A copy of Alexander of Villedieu's *Doctrinale,* one of the most popular textbooks of the late Middle Ages, is twice glossed with the definition of poetry that Matthew gives in his *Art* (I, 1).[46] Writing about 1280, Hugh of Trimberg—after mentioning Homer, Pindar, Priscian, Donatus, and Boethius among eminent authors—lists in the same company "the sincere Matthew," "the outstanding Alain," and "the far from ordinary Geoffrey."[47] Matthew's *Art of Versification* has survived in five manuscripts, and many other manuscripts contain in whole or in part the poetic examples that he composed for that work to illustrate his teaching.[48]

In his famous Wharton lecture, "Chaucer and the Rhetoricians," J. M. Manly shows Chaucer's debt to Matthew and Geoffrey.[49] Faral has documented the influence of the twelfth- and thirteenth-century arts of poetry on later Latin literature and vernacular poetry, particularly French.[50] Further testimony to the influence of Matthew and the other late medieval theoreticians is given by Curtius, who asserts, "Dante's poetic and rhetoric are based upon them."[51] Curtius also notes that in the *De vulgari eloquentia* (II, 4, 2) Dante recommends adherence to the *doctrinatae poetriae,* and says,

> Of these poetics, Dante names only Horace's. But since he uses the plural, he has others in mind too—namely, the Latin poetics of the twelfth and thirteenth centuries. That he knew them and guided himself by them, we have already learned from his use of periphrase and *annominatio.*[52]

Also one should note that Matthew's statement, "There are three qualities which distinguish poetry: polished language (*verba polita*), figurative expression (*dicendi color*), and the inner sentiment (*interior favus*)" (III, 1), is very close to Dante's view of poetry,[53] a fact his critics have ignored. C. S. Lewis has indicated how Matthew's five ways of ending a poem have been followed by such English authors as Chaucer, Gower, and Hawes.[54]

Many modern critics have, however, tended to disparage Matthew. As we have seen, Raby can say, "With Matthew poetry is nothing more than a school exercise"[55]; and C. S. Baldwin dismisses much of the *Art of Versification* as "purely verbal."[56] Helen Waddell, who must have forgotten Geoffrey's *Documentum,* writes, "Matthew of Vendôme is responsible for perhaps the dullest Art of Poetry that ever has been written."[57] Hauréau, who calls Matthew "un des professeurs les plus célèbres et un des versificateurs les plus féconds du XIIe siècle," has an even harsher judgment to make upon the *Art:* "Au point de vue de la science, à peu prés nulles; au point de vue du talent, médiocres."[58] M.-D. Chenu, on the other hand, cites "Matthew of Vendôme [who] exalted the role and excellence of metaphor" as evidence of "the symbolist mentality of the century."[59] Winthrop Wetherbee, moreover, reminds us that Matthew's "excesses must not blind us to the positive side of the *Ars versificatoria* or lead us to dismiss Matthew as an amusing grotesque. His concern with language is real, and in certain ways reflects the concerns of the Chartrians."[60] In a more recent study Douglas Kelly has noted the relevance of Matthew's poetics, particularly with reference to the *Roman de la Rose.*[61]

In evaluating Matthew's work, one must consider the audience for whom he wrote. Matthew's book is intended for boys (*pueri*) to use in the study of grammar in the early stages of education. Grammar, of course, included verse composition; the important point is that the *Art of Versification* was not written for a university class in creative writing. The students who turned to Matthew's text would find practical, straightforward help in composing the sort of descriptive verses demanded in school exercises.

The *Art* answers the question, How does one describe a person or an event? Matthew gives some rather explicit instructions, again seeking to teach the student to write within an accepted literary tradition. He points out that the purpose of descriptions is to praise or to blame and that details to be used in a description should be chosen in light of this purpose. Description is a matter of assigning attributes, and he explains the sorts of attributes that can be assigned to a person or an action. He points out that the kind of descriptions his students are writing are idealized portraits and indicates the qualities that ought to be ascribed to various classes of persons. Students learn how to go about telling what they should about their subjects.

Not only does the *Art* instruct the student in the vocabulary of poetry and the substance or subject matter of poetry, it also offers instruction in how to ornament poetry by using such devices as figures and tropes. Matthew's students were learning to write poetry within a convention that highly prized ornamentation through rhetorical devices. The section on figures and tropes in the *Art* is designed to show the student how to master these methods of making verse elegant.

If much of Matthew's concern is verbal, that is because the writing problems to which he was addressing himself were largely verbal. This verbal character of his instructions in the art of versifying is due partly to the poetic conventions within which he was operating and partly to his audience. His students were writing short, descriptive poems based either upon previously versified material or upon prose accounts they had before them. One would not learn from the *Art of Versification* how to write epics or lyrics. One might learn how to become reasonably proficient in writing Latin elegiacs acceptable to the literary taste of the age. Or in Matthew's words:

> This little book instructs boys about verses; it takes
> Its name from that fact; it can teach the major ideas. (IV, 51)

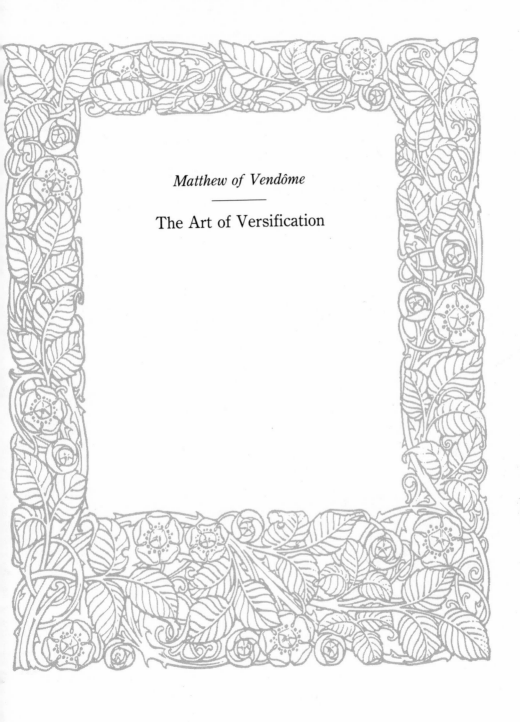

Matthew of Vendôme

The Art of Versification

PROLOGUE

1.   Let the spirit of envy cease, let no enemy
Gnash at this introductory work of Vendôme's.

Lest I seem to enlarge the fringes of my garments,[1] I have put off this proposed work for some time. But since delaying is the stepmother to the fulfillment of promises made, "I would not want to seem to be dissimulating about my own talents or to be following a plan of action convenient to myself alone" (Hor., *Ep.*, I, 9, 9)[2] in the considered judgment of reason. Rather I have desired to translate my promises into accomplished fact according to the meagerness of my slight talent. Thus I offer this work for the advancement of learning, for the increase of knowledge, as fodder for envy, torment for enmity, and food for detraction. **2.** Since I am offering the truce of reasoned judgment to my detractors, let them not in presumptuous attack rashly prejudge my little book without so much as even consulting the domain of reason or having studied what I have written. Therefore, since a period of silence is food for sensible speech and "rashness serves all things ill" (Stat., *Theb.*, X, 704), let my acknowledged enemy Rufinus, a reproach to men and rejected of the people,[3] place a guard at his mouth and a door all around his lips; nor let him, because of puffed-up envy, cast headlong vituperation at my pages without stopping to think, rather let him, sporting with his wench, embrace his red-haired Thaïs. Indeed:

3.   If Rufinus gnaws away at my verses, his red color will
Become the index of his baseness. His words match his skin,
His tongue plays with a tongue's color, for a faith
Red in color throbs within the heart of Rufus.[4]

Truly I am not envious:

> If she has borne up me, a scholar, for pay
> Let the red she-goat bear Rufus as her buck.

If one cannot bite, one ought to bark less loudly. **4.** Also, the novelty of this little book ought not to be ascribed to presumption because neither a desire for acclaim nor a display of empty pride set this book in motion; rather it is offered as some sort of instruction for the less ad-

[25]

vanced. Thus let the intention of the author win favor even if the execution of his book cannot. **5.** Therefore, because I am held in the bond of a promise and "since it always does harm to put off what has been begun" (Luc., *Phars.,* I, 281), I would not want to seem to act like the procrastinating bumpkin described by Horace:

> The bumpkin waits for the river to run out, yet on it glides,
> And on it will glide, rolling its flood forever. (*Ep. I,* 2, 42)

"Since a fit hour for my stories has come" (Ovid, *Met.,* V, 499), let Rufus burst his sides with envy.[5] I begin my introductory little work with this pact: that if anything in the following treatment should lack even a spark of charm, whoever repays evil for good and returns to me the gift of shameful retaliation by presuming to break into loud laughter shall have his barren and fruitless loquacity punished by "the arrow that flies by day or by the pestilence that walks in darkness." (Ps. 90:6). **6.** Although in writing verses I have chosen for myself my home-grown path since "it is shameful to travel a well-worn path" (Luc., *Phars.,* II, 446) and "wretched to seek fame with another's work" (Juv., *Sat.,* VIII, 76), I do not, however, presume to disparage the skill of others with censorious revision. On the contrary, if anyone seeking some fault will disparage the following work as negligent or— what is easy—if he will be prejudiced against me on account of my lack of skill as a versifier, "I neither wait for the slow nor run after the speedy" (Hor., *Ep.,* I, 2, 71). **7.** Furthermore, let those who patch together rags[6] be excluded from a scrutiny of this work. For though many versifiers are called, few are chosen.[7] Certain persons who shall remain nameless, however, relying only on the title poet, pant after the number of verses rather than the elegance of the verses numbered. They turn out their ragged verses, attempting to make a unified poem out of an assortment of trifles, like "a tree that forms shade from its trunk rather than from its leaves" (Luc., *Phars.,* I, 140). These ill-sorted verses dare never appear in public but clamor out among themselves:

> We are mere ciphers born to consume the fruits of earth. (Hor.,
> *Ep.,* I, 2, 27)

I

WRITING OF DESCRIPTIONS

1. Since our immediate purpose is to give an introduction to verse, a general definition that applies to all verse ought to be given. Verse is metrical discourse advancing in cadenced periods with the restraint that meter demands and made charming by a graceful marriage of words and by flowers of thought. It contains in itself nothing deficient and nothing redundant. For it is not the accumulation of words, the counting of feet, and knowledge of meter that constitute verse but the elegant combination of words, the vivid presentation of relevant qualities, and the carefully noted epithets of each single thing.

2. An epithet, moreover, shows an attribute belonging to some noun; it may signify something good, bad, or indifferent. It signifies something bad in:

Old Laertes, (Ovid, *Her.*, I, 98)

since we have the teaching of Horace that:

Many ills encumber an old man, (*Poet.*, 169)

or something good in:

The youth Telemachus, (Ovid, *Her.*, I, 98)

since "the heart of a youth is easily made glad" (Maxim., *Eleg.*, I, 105). It signifies the indifferent in:

The white swan sings at the fords of the Meander, (Ovid, *Her.*, VII, 2)

since being black or white does not indicate good or bad.

3. When the techniques of versification are put into practice, the material is introduced in two ways which can be very effective. There are four other ways of beginning,[8] but I pass over these as rejected even by the bleary-eyed and barbers.[9] Thus I offer the listener only two choices.

4. The first way of beginning is to use the figure *zeugma. Zeugma* is making a single verb serve as the predicate of different clauses.

5. There are three varieties of *zeugma: zeugma* at the beginning of a series, in the middle, or at the end.

6. *Zeugma* at the beginning occurs when a verb used in the first of a series of clauses has its meaning understood for the succeeding clauses in that series. As in Ovid:

> Cold things strove with hot, and moist with dry, soft things
> With hard, things having weight with weightless things. (*Met.,* I,
> 19)

7. And to use my own example, if one undertakes to write approvingly about the female sex, he might begin this way:

> Callisto is renowned for zeal with the bow,
> Bright with the image of nature in bloom, rich in ancestors.

8. Or if one writes disapprovingly, he might begin with the same figure:

> Medea is the dregs of womanhood, the downfall of justice,
> The shame of nature, a foul plague.

9. One begins a piece praising or blaming a man in a similar manner. One might write approvingly:

> Caesar is famed as a warrior, as a friend of honor,
> As wise in counsel, as master of Rome.

10. Or disapprovingly:

> Verres is polluted by the vice of theft, destitute of honor,
> Prone to plunder, a sluggard in war.

11. *Zeugma* at the end is using in a final clause a verb whose meaning is understood in preceding clauses—thus:

> My master, my husband, my brother you were. (Ovid, *Her.,* III,
> 52)

I do not want to appear lavish with examples. So since an example from a recognized author has already been given, one of my own must suffice. This one praises the subject:

> Through charm of manner, through splendor of face,
> Through pleasant conversation, through glory of birth Ino shines.

12. *Zeugma* in the middle occurs when a verb appears only in the middle clause of a series but is also the predicate of clauses that precede and follow it. As in Statius:

> Now shield against shield, boss against boss, threatening sword
> Clashes against sword, foot against foot, lance against lance.
> (*Theb.,* VIII, 398)

Or another example describes that earth-born seed of Cadmus who destroyed one another:

> They perish, their beginning their end, their doing
> Is their undoing, their first day their last day.

13. One can begin in a second way, using *hypozeuxis,* which is the opposite of *zeugma.* In *hypozeuxis* each clause has its own verb expressed. As in Statius:

> She yearns for war, and she loosens
> Her jaws, and she trims her talons. (*Theb.,* II, 130)

Or one might begin the praise of a king or prelate in this way. An example of my own is:

> Excellence in conduct glorifies Agenor, manliness makes him
> Famous, wealth marks him, his reputation makes him happy.

One might write similarly of a woman:

> Gracious conduct marks Penelope, regal form
> Distinguishes her, great wealth enriches her.

14. *Hypozeuxis,* moreover (to repeat what was said earlier), is a figure of speech opposite to *zeugma* because in *zeugma,* as can be seen from the examples given above, one verb serves as the predicate of several clauses. In *hypozeuxis,* on the other hand, each clause has its own verb.

15. In addition to these figures, in beginning a work one should use *metonymy* fairly often, which is assigning the container to the thing contained (or vice versa), as in:

> Thebes celebrates the Bacchic rites; a reverent throng
> Crowds the places sacred to the god, it honors anew
> Her shrines, it burns the sacred incense.

Lucan affords an example of the thing contained used for the container:

> The people of the Seine that excel
> In whirling their mounts with curved bits. (*Phars.,* I, 425)

Here the river Seine is used for the region in which it is contained.

16. I turn now to the use of general sentiments or proverbs. Just as one may use *zeugma* or *hypozeuxis* for a beginning, so may he also begin with a general proverb, that is, universal sentiments in which custom reinforces belief, in which common opinion agrees, and in which the purity of unalloyed truth inheres. **17.** If, for example, the uncertainty of Fortune is treated, one may begin with a proverb such as this:

The deceitful favor of Fortune gives the nod to ruin.
The one certainty in Chance is uncertainty.
The wheel of Fortune is fickle, mobile;
Indeed it is faith not to have faith in chance.
"All things concerning man are held suspended by a thread
And suddenly those things which were firmly held fall." (Ovid,
    Pont., IV, 3, 35)

18. If the misfortunes of love are discussed, it is possible to assign a proverb to them; thus:

When cruel love rules, reason wanders in exile,
Injustice is the order of the day.
Love, which neither respects rank in men nor spares
Even the gods, makes all liberty subject to itself.

Or as in Ovid:

Love rules and holds sway over even the supreme gods. (*Her.,*
    IV, 12)

19. Concerning the slowness of a promise which tortures the expectation, one might write thus:

Favor is to be given promptly
And the slow hand of the giver is the stepmother of merit. (Matt.,
    Tob., 777)[10]

Or as in Lucan:

Let it be done quickly, whatsoever you make ready. (*Phars.,* II,
    14)

Or according to the Apostle: "God loves a cheerful giver" (2 Cor. 9:7).
20. Concerning the imperfection of happiness which is a trial to human life, one might begin thus:

Imperfection, as envious comrade, attends human affairs;
All prosperity lacks completeness.

Or as Horace puts it:

No life is blessed in every way. (*Od.,* II, 16, 28)

Or Cato:

No one lives without guilt. (*Dist.,* I, 5)

21. Concerning ingenuity which affliction ordinarily increases:

Grief increases the resources of ingenuity; an ingenious
Carefulness discerns more in hard times. (Matt., *Milo,* 91; *Pyr. and
    Th.,* 77)

Or as Ovid says:

> Cunning thrives on deep grief,
> And ingenuity comes with trouble. (*Met.,* VI, 574)

22. Concerning changeableness of mind, one might begin:

> Changing the mind shows a loss of faith;
> It is an unusual faith that beats in a fickle breast.

23. Concerning the effect of wisdom which judges the outcome of things, one might say:

> It judges goals—what and where it may reap.

Or as Lucan says:

> This was the character, the austere rule of inflexible Cato,
> To be moderate and to hold fast to the end. (*Phars.,* II, 380)

24. Concerning the power of fear:

> Fear conjures up whatever is evil; it prophesies things
> To be feared and foretells disaster in unsettled times. (Matt., *Milo,* 97)

Or as in Statius:

> Fear is the worst guide, for in consternation
> It turns here and there. (*Theb.,* III, 6)

25. Concerning the presumptuous destruction of nature:

> A silly presumption that hurts, is deceived, errs,
> Is to hope to destroy natural good.

Or as Horace says:

> You may drive nature out with a pitchfork,
> But she will keep on coming right back. (*Ep.,* I, 10, 24)

26. The effect of custom:

> Custom tastes of nature; an unglazed jar
> Does not lose the taste of what it first held.

Or in Horace:

> A jar will keep for a long time,
> The odor of what was steeped in it when new. (*Ep.,* I, 2, 69)

Whatever a jar holds when new, it smells of when old.
27. Or, since the fame of a person is nothing without virtue, thus:

> Virtue enobles the spirit; if virtue is gone,
> The distinction of nobility wanders in exile.

Or as Claudian says:

> One should glory in honor, not name.
> There is but one virtue, a noble heart. (Claud., VIII, 220
>   [*Honor.*])

28. And since sin is most evident through the position of the sinner:

> The fame of the sinner enlarges the sin;
> The distinction of a silly fame defames the fault.

Or as in Juvenal:

> The guilt of the sin grows with the fame of the sinner. (*Sat.,*
>   VIII, 140)

29. Concerning the fury of slaves:

> A rage that knows not law nor limit nor honor
> Abounds in the curses of slaves.

As Claudian says:

> None is crueller than a man who has risen from a low estate
> To a high one. He strikes all about him, for he fears
> All about him. He rages at all so that they may know that he can.
> No wild beast is so hideous as the fury of a slave vented
> Upon the backs of free men. He has groaned as they do now,
> And he cannot refrain from inflicting a punishment
> Which he himself has suffered. The memory of his own master
> Makes him hate the man he flogs. (Claud., XVIII, 181 [*Eutr.*])

Many other proverbs might be used in this manner.

30. Whether one uses *zeugma* or *hypozeuxis* for a beginning, three faulty styles are attendant on the beginning and on the working out of the material, which according to Horace ought especially to be avoided, namely, the drifting and slack, the turgid and inflated, the dry and bloodless.[11] **31.** For one who sets out on the middle style in diction is either carried away into high-flown language or sinks into diction too common and ordinary. Thus he incurs the fault that is called drifting and slack, that is, lacking in cohesiveness, so that:

> The beginning does not agree with the middle
> Nor the middle with the end.[12]

Horace, moreover, condemns this fault, saying:

> Feeling and vigor desert one striving for smoothness. (*Poet.,* 26)

32. The second fault occurs when one using needlessly high-flown words and ornate language achieves only vain obscurity because no ending of the discourse seems able to match the splendor of the beginning. Horace condemns this fault, saying of such a writer:

> Promising great things, he merely grows bombastic. (*Poet.,* 27)

And elsewhere he quotes the turgid and inflated beginning used by the cyclic poet:

> Of Priam's fate and famous war I will sing. (*Poet.,* 137)

Horace immediately rebukes him for this presumptuous beginning:

> What shall this boaster write further that shall be in
> Keeping with such inflated language? Mountains will
> Labor only to give birth to a ridiculous mouse. (*Poet.,* 138)

33. The third fault is a dry and bloodless style that results when one using excessively low speech neglects flowers of diction and sweetness of thought. Choosing a metaphor from sailing, Horace condemns this fault also:

> Overcautious and fearful of the storm, he creeps along the coast.
> (*Poet.,* 28)

34. Certainly, one ought to observe uniformity in embellishments and propriety in language, for as Horace says:

> Don't as an imitator jump into a deep well from which shame
> Or the demands of your work will keep you from moving a foot.
> (*Poet.,* 134)

But while observing propriety in delineation of character, let the material as it is worked out:

> Remain to the end even as it came forth
> At the first and have it self-consistent. (*Poet.,* 127)

Let the writing be neither scanty nor prolix.

35. There are other faults which Horace, in the beginning of the *Art of Poetry,* teaches one to shun. But to avoid prolixity, which is the stepmother of memory, I skip these at present and leave the investigation of this aspect of poetry to the diligence of my listeners.

36. In the working out of the material, moreover, one ought to pay strict attention to differences in verb tense lest divergent changes in style occur. When there is a difference in verb tenses, there is a mismatching of sentiments, a fault which certainly ought to be avoided unless there is an overriding reason:

> Unless a knot worthy of such a deliverer occurs. (Hor., *Poet.,* 191)

For when the compulsion of necessity is felt, any rule loses force. If one writes about the past or the future, he ought to use the same care as when writing in the present tense and active voice. For whoever uses present-tense verbs proceeds succinctly and briefly, and straightforward brevity pleases an audience.

37. An improper word order ought to be avoided, lest the words of even short phrases become too complex and involved. Such a confusion of words is the stepmother of understanding and a hindrance to learning. So that syntactically related words are close to each other, the versifier ought to order poetry to avoid that fault called *cacosyntheton,* that is, improper position of words. For *kacos* means "bad," and *synthesis* comes from *syn,* that is, "along with" or "at the same time," and *thesis,* which is "position."

38. Further, one must decide whether or not to describe the character about whom he is writing. In many cases a description of the person is fitting, in many superfluous. **39.** For instance, if one writes about the strength, steadfastness of mind, devotion to honesty, and refusal to be servile of a certain person, as we have Lucan writing of the austerity of Cato (*Phars.,* II, 380), then one ought to describe the various virtues of Cato, so that when the audience has had set before them the fastidiousness of Cato's habits and the special quality of his virtue, they can more easily understand what follows about the heedlessness of Caesar and Cato's concern for liberty. **40.** Or again, if one writes about the power of love—how, for example, Jupiter burned with love for Callisto—then the audience ought to be given a foretaste of such exquisite feminine beauty, so that having a picture of such beauty in their minds, they would find it reasonably believable that a heart as great as Jupiter's could be heated up over the charms of a mere mortal. For it ought to be made clear what a wealth of charms it was that drove Jupiter to so vile an act.

41. Further, one should describe not only the qualities which a person has but also those qualities which differentiate that person from others. One should pay attention to characteristics such as status, age, occupation, sex, geography, native land, and other qualities which Tully calls personal attributes (*De inventione,* I, 24–25). **42.** Horace points out differences in characteristics, writing:

> It will make a big difference whether the speaker is Davus or a
> hero

(a difference in status),

> A hoary old man or one still blooming with the flower of youth

(a difference in age),

> An upper-class lady or a busy nurse

(a difference in status, this time among women),

> A wandering peddler or a small farmer

(a difference in occupation),

> A Colchian or an Assyrian

(a difference in nationality),

> One raised in Thebes or in Argos

(a difference in citizenship) (*Poet.,* 114 ff.). **43.** Horace explains why such distinct attributes should be noted, saying:

> Lest by chance we give a youth the part of old age
> Or a mere boy that of a man, we shall linger long
> Over traits considered appropriate for a given age. (*Poet.,* 176)

44. Any person ought to be described by epithets which show the dominant traits on which most of his reputation rests, just as Horace says:

> If as a writer you depict Achilles full of honor, make him
> Impatient, quick-tempered, ruthless, fierce; make him claim
> He is subject to no law. Make him decide everything with arms.
> (*Poet.,* 120)

45. Moreover, the sort of words a person uses when speaking ought to conform to one's facial expression as well as to his fortunes. For example:

> Sad words fit a dejected expression, threatening ones
> An angry countenance; playful words fit
> A light mood, serious ones a grave mood. (*Poet.,* 105)

Horace goes on to indicate why it is important to fit the words to the speaker:

> If a speaker's words do not fit his fortunes,
> The Roman commoners and nobles alike will break out laughing.
> (*Poet.,* 112)

Here he seems to have particularly in mind the methods employed in reading aloud.[13]

46. One description may be of the pastor of a church, one of an emperor, another of a girl, another of an old woman, another of a middle-aged woman, another of a concubine, another of a serving girl, another of a young boy, another of an adolescent, another of an old man, another of a freedman, another of a bond servant. In fact, descriptions of a wide variety of characters may be used. These are what Horace calls the colors of a work (*Poet.,* 86). **47.** Now, since the best way to make an idea clear is through easily understood examples, I will give some examples of descriptions of various sorts of persons.

These examples are given merely to instruct; and if faults are apparent in the following verses, I hope no nitpicker will take delight in taunting me with being a mere poetaster. **48.** For:

> At times even good Homer nods. (*Poet.,* 359)
> Nor will the bow always hit the mark it threatens. (*Poet.,* 350)

Horace, moreover, offers me this solace against detractors, saying:

> When the beauties in a poem are more numerous, I shall
> Not be offended at a few blots which carelessness let fall
> Or human nature was powerless to prevent. (*Poet.,* 351)

Indeed, fault lies not in committing an error, but in persisting in it. As Horace says:

> To have been foolish is not shameful,
> But not to cut short the folly is. (*Ep.,* I, 14, 36)

49. Thus let nothing in the following descriptions be understood as asserting my poetic ability; they are given merely for the sake of example.

50. The world looks to the Pope as an example;
In him honesty shines, reason reigns, order flourishes.
Dutiful in religion and modest in voice, nourisher of
Virtue, provident of counsel, the crown of the world,
He is zealous to hold forth what should be held forth.   5
He does not change his words to please his hearers.
Reason is exalted when he leads; his gentle temper
Remains settled; his gracious piety blossoms into peacemaking.
His way of life does not smack of earthly affairs;
Beholding God, he eschews man's sinful pursuits.   10
He succors the sorrowful, ministers to the miserable,
Strives for lawfulness, reproves the reprobate, and fosters justice.
The Pope teaches what ought to be taught, prohibits what
Ought to be prohibited, and condemns sin. He holds spiritual
Sway. He binds and frees souls; binding and freeing souls,   15
He plays the part of a heavenly shepherd. He watches over us
His children, his sheep, the limbs of his body, as the head
Over bodily members, the father children, the shepherd sheep.
An assembly of virtues is at strife in the Pope;
Virtue vies with virtue for the place of honor.   20
Each virtue of this holy man insists it stands foremost.
Contesting virtues sue for sole possession of the Father.
Temperance is eager to supplant justice and
Gentle piety claims the Holy Father all for herself.
A fourth, wisdom, strives to surpass the first three.   25
Virtue with sister virtue, gift with gift, all vie for the Father.
His laws are firm, his pity mild, his temperance soothing.
His wisdom guides each virtue in rectitude.

On these four the Pope stands foursquare.
This foursome makes him firm and his faith enduring.   30
Supported by this foursome, he does not stray into guilty ways
And has not in his mind to be unmindful of God.
The Pope rules rulers, as their lord asserts his lordship;
He commands harsh princes to command by fixed law.
He goes beyond human evaluation; casting off   35
The affections of human frailty, he outshines humanness.
Pressing beyond common humanity, he reaches beyond the earth
Where he sojourns to ponder the way to his heavenly home.
He is eager to exchange the changeable for the changeless,
The vain for the certain, earth for heaven, a hostel   40
For a home. His holy mind loathes its vessel of corruption;
His lofty soul laments being bound in fetters of flesh.
The body, his bride, does not diminish the dowry of the spirit;
His spirit, the bridegroom, seeks to enrich his body, the bride.
His mind thirsts for its heavenly home; as our shepherd,   45
His body is a guest on earth, his spirit a resident of heaven.
Guilt does not darken his pious heart with impious assault,
Nor is it able to devalue his value.
He is good; he is better; he is best; in fact,
He merits a fourth degree of comparison.   50

51. Caesar's steadfastness shines in battle; he brooks
No opposition; he breaks the brave; he tames the fierce.
He remains dutiful in adversity; he shows himself
An enemy to our enemies; yet he is mild to the mild.
As the ideal knight he outshines other leaders in manliness,   5
Outstrips them in rewards, and exceeds them in honors.
He hastens to face obstacles; he sighs for
Soldierly duties, chafes at rest, and flies to arms.
He thirsts for war and does not know the meaning of retreat.
His sword is now in the enemy flank, now at the back of a rout.   10
He delights to trust in the sword; there justice is measured
By an iron judge. He shows the way with flashing sword.
Fortune nods at the nod of Caesar,
Who holds two-faced fortune in derision.
He rises to master hardships, nor do   15
Wintry blasts of angry fortune dampen his stern
Countenance. He curbs the fierce and strengthens the meek.
Separating sloth from peace in the scales of justice,
Dutifully he combines law with temperance, while he tempers
The rod of judgment with gentle compassion.   20
He serves in this manner lest compassion overcome law
And lest the law deny works of compassion.
The responsibility of power does not impoverish his judgment;
Each of his virtues performs its appointed role.
His natural talents thrive; his skills are not exiled.   25
Nor does zeal drive out his imperial discipline.
No wish for the scepter darkens his bright character,
No distinction of mind, no honor of birth, no mass of wealth.

No thirst for popular acclaim mars his integrity, for
The flavor of integrity makes his rule delightful.   30
Slayer Caesar lives up to his name;[14] his slaying
Hand makes clear the significance of his name.
For him it is rest to be deprived of rest and labor
To be deprived of labor. He suffers if he cannot suffer.
He is the man whose terror conquers from afar, whose praise   35
Fame's reports beggar, whose very name wins battles.
Caesar's presence carries the day for Caesar;
The shadow of his name overcomes armed might. Vigorous,
Indomitable, warlike, he presses foes, conducts battles,
Urges on his cohorts, one with the sword, one with rigor,   40
One with fear. Audacious in arms, eager for glory, stern
Of countenance, he stands midst blood, strife, threats.
Vigilant, active, quick, he meets battle with hope,
Doubts with confidence, flight with a sword.
Manliness endows his limbs with strength,   45
Fame his toil with praise, resolution his mind
With assurance. He is the best of daring leaders,
One who has enriched Rome with many a tribute.

52. Ulysses is renowned for his speech,
Celebrated for his judgment, famed for his manner.
Keen in speech, prudent in judgment, mighty in cunning,
Ulysses delights in a pleasing tongue. This man from Ithaca
Ranks first in genius; strong in mind, prudent in word,   5
Mighty in cunning, he is ever mindful of honesty.
Lest the glory of his intellect be dimmed, he embellishes
With flourishing elegance what lesser men speak plainly.
Lest his mighty tongue be divorced from sound judgment,
He weds the judgment of integrity to the words of his tongue.   10
He couples genius with zeal like a husband zealous
That his pleasure bear fruit in offspring.
When judgment has spoken, genius conceives ideas, reason
Leads him to sort out ideas, and resolution nourishes them.
His genius sows, his zeal cultivates, his ability tends,   15
His reason weeds; as servant to these his tongue sounds forth.
Judgment is the forerunner and reason is the guide;
These two make his tongue master of his thoughts.
Not a cell of Ulysses's brain can be called wanting;
Imagination, reason, memory are each active in its role.   20
The first perceives, the middle one discerns, the third retains;
The first comprehends, the middle one judges, the third unites all.
The first sows, the middle one tills, the third reaps.
The first reports, the middle one savors, the third holds all.
Imagination serves the other two; it is the door for ideas,   25
Reason is their guest chamber, and memory their permanent
    dwelling.
Imagination admits them at the door; reason observes
And judges them; memory bars the door against their flight.
Reason stands in the center and salutes the other two:

The open door at the front of the head and the barred one at the
    back.   30
Ulysses excels nature in his virtue and the inner man
Is the faithful master of the outer man.
Just as he exceeds mankind in his manner, his judgment
Outweighs the glory of nature that fostered him.
He ponders doubtful cases with wisdom, weighing   35
Just against unjust cause in the scales of justice.
Not until he has weighed the rightness of a deed
Does his hand, the friend of his mind's deliberation, act.
Sorting arguments into their parts, he brings opposites together
And does deeds that correspond to his words.   40
He hands over his purposes to speedy action; the acts of his hands,
The revealer of his mind, agree with the words of his mouth.
His youthfulness does not lessen the force of his intellect;
Indeed, he is a stripling with the wisdom of a graybeard.
His mature judgment belies his age. His counsel worthy   45
Of elders shows a youth wise beyond his years.
His excellence leads him beyond youthful desires;
His keen mind gives him authority beyond his years.
Mature judgment holds his age in check and
His mind dazzles as it surpasses his tender age.   50
No chill blast of arrogance spoils the bloom of his spirit.
No reproach dims his glory, nor chance his strength; no men
Of wavering mind grasp his fixed goals, no rigid minds
His many shifts, no trivial minds his grave designs.
Neither the cannibal king nor Circe nor Charybdis   55
Was powerful enough to shake Ulysses's iron will.
He overcomes hardships, promotes laws, increases trust,
As one brave, rational, upright. Prudent, fluent, powerful,
He ennobles, adorns, dignifies the thoughts of his heart,
The words of his mouth, the work of his hands,   60
By his mind, his gracefulness, and his deeds.
In eloquence he is a Cicero, in war a Caesar, in judgment
An Adrastus, in wisdom a Nestor, in discipline a Cato.

53. A roaming buffoon, a gluttonous parasite, an offscouring of
The masses, Davus is a sickening pest, disgraceful in his deeds.
A fomenter of crime, an overthrower of justice, a mocker of
The laws, the very dregs of mankind, he is strong in fraud.
A child of wantonness, poor in truth, rich in trivia,   5
Deformed in body and poisoned in mind,
He is a Tersites in form, an Argus in deceit, a Tyresias
In honor, a Verres in crime, a Sinon in fraud.
Ignorant of virtue, he is an eager servant of vice.
This enemy of nature damns the just and   10
Oppresses the honest. His evil genius
Disposes everything to some infamous use.
Criminality is innate in Davus. In him every deceit
Is met; he makes every foul business his business.
Prone to treachery, quick to anger, blind to public good,   15

He thinks himself injured if he misses a chance to do ill.
Breathing illicit adventures, this troubler of the peace,
This destroyer of loves strives to be known as an evil
Man, a more evil man, the most evil man. Full of rumor,
Always mouthing nonsense, he conceals the good and makes   20
Known what a decent man would conceal. He is a cesspool
Of immorality, a well of debauchery; he is no ignoramus
Ignorant of his ignobility. His mind, steeped in evil,
Must own his faults; his hand can master every sin.
He is so habituated to vice that he finds it hard   25
To break the habit, so he goes his habitual evil way.
His habits mark him as wicked by nature; he is a
Son of perdition. Davus is unable not to be evil;
Evil by nature, he reckons himself unnatural
If ever he acts in accord with man's better nature.   30
Who is destitute of faithfulness and righteousness,
Who works only to defraud, who seizes any evil occasion;
Whose honor is that he lacks honor, whose steadfastness
Is to be without steadfastness, whose faith is faithlessness;
To whom it is sin to shun sin, to whom it is villainy   35
To lack villainy, to whom it is shame to be ashamed;
Whom fear reveals to be a scared rabbit, whom plunder shows
To be a lion, whom sex shows to be an old goat and theft
A fox, whom greed shows to be a wolf; in whom reason, as
A guide, goes begging, in whom virtue, as a leader, is exiled,   40
In whom faithfulness has wasted away, in whom good has fled
In the face of evil, peace in the midst of fury, piety in
The face of impiety. I have declined Davus; the vocative
I decline to decline. If I address him, words stick in my throat.
Davus, the unparalleled scum of the earth, is fit only for jail; 45
No, he is fit to be struck by Jove's forked bolt, fit to die.
A man of no charms, he repays love with hate, trust with
Deceit, gifts with theft, kindness by being a pest.
Behold this mass of evil—a depraved mind, a debauched
Body, a false tongue, and a fraudulent hand.   50
A shell as rotten as the kernel shows him no hypocrite;
Not one of his deeds is less scandalous than the next.
Too deceitful to allow his outward mien to reflect his inner
Mind, Davus affects a sort of metonymy of the spirit.
He is gay when sorrowful, down-in-the-mouth when happy.   55
This man is a lumpish social outcast, a shame to nature,
A burden to the very earth, a bottomless pit of depravity,
A stinking dung heap. He is goaded along by envy.
He must share the feasts of others, invited or not.
He dashes to the table, picks the best meat, spurns   60
The vegetables. Only after he is stuffed is this
Friend of the belly slowed down. It is worse than
Bad, sadder than sad to see this glutton gobble
Delicacy after delicacy and never count the cost.
He drains the goblets, then the pitchers brimming with   65
Choice wines; the rich table is reduced to poverty.

His god is his belly, kitchens his temples, a cook
His priest, and cooking aromas his incense.
He sits at a plate and gulps a poor feast, as his quick
Fingers prove themselves a true friend to his belly. 70
He busies himself equally at meat platter and sauce pot,
Making a trumpet of his rear and answering this tune with a belch.
In fact, after he has attacked a dinner, his stuffed gut
Contains so much wind that he is able to play Aeolus.
Davus, belching and farting, is like a broken prison 75
No longer able to contain those things
Which most need to be contained.
He turns to lewdness as a foul passion suffuses his genitals,
Causing love's orbs to bulge and Venus's lance to stiffen.
Yet before the lengthy member of this dactyl can pierce home,
The short syllables shake and destroy the enterprise. 80
His wickedness shows him a slave to madness,
And his acts make clear the depth of his depravity.
Seeking out every source of sensual gratification,
He is inflamed at the sight of a naked body.
This man is a rebel against nature,
One who travels across thresholds forbidden to natural tastes.
He corrupts the innocent; he makes the particular vices 85
Of his own evil heart flourish in a thousand innocent breasts.
He is a bundle of sins, a fog in the midst of light,
A thunderstorm in the marketplace, a pestilence, an open privy.
Poisonous, depraved, slothful, he destroys happiness with strife,
Perverts lawful procedure with fraud, vexes honest men with
    guile. 90
Stripped of all esteem he rejoices in strife;
Lacking any claim to virtue he abounds in ill temper;
Empty of even common decency he thrives on treachery.
Quarrels, abuse, deceit he seeks out, employs, embraces;
And he distorts, spurns, hates agreement, religion, lawfulness.
At his birth Virtue recognized her enemy and said,
"War, I see war brewing for me." (Ovid., *Rem.*, I., 2) 95

54. Cartula writes a simple poetry which glides to the ear
Of the listener in plain but melodious style.
The friend of literature rejoices at this rough
Style which receives its strength from its sincerity.
Written from his heart, his verse sparkles; 5
The contents glorify the container.
Hail, teacher, mirror of the fatherland, ornament
To the city, exemplar of honesty, spark of industry,
May your memory never fade. I give thanks to you
As the vase to the potter, the rivulet to the river, 10
The waves to the sea. I rejoice because your praise
Is on all men's lips, because your fame is certain,
Because your worth shines out, because you are wise.
Your wisdom discounts faint praises of envious critics.
In your way of life you surpass other men. Your excellent 15

Character overcomes frailties inherent in human nature.
I long to see you; weary, I desire your refreshing mind,
As shipwrecks desire port and hell-parched souls water.
Mirror for mankind, be mindful of your student
Who holds fast what you taught him as a youth. On the   20
Day you were born Reason acknowledged you as her
Child saying, "I see my sway made sure."
I am silent. A terse brevity suffices.
If a poem lacks brevity, it lacks poetry.[15]

55. Marcia outshines all in virtues; she overflows
With delights of manner; she goes beyond mere duty.
By example she fosters womanly virtue, having no part in
Pride, ignorant of unchastity, free from deceit.
She is marked by innumerable gifts, modest   5
In word, prudent in counsel, strong in mind.
She scorns lewd gestures, she strives to deny base
Nature, she spurns all hints of sensuality.
She makes the weak sex strong and rejects feminine
Frauds; she smacks of discretion and shines with   10
Faithfulness. Her manner graces nature's infirmity;
This bold matron puts innate evil to flight.
She is matron in name only; her spirit rejects
An epithet of Nature and cancels all deceit.
The beauty of her face bespeaks her excellent worth;   15
Her expression is the prophet of honorable intent.
No lightness of mind marks her as a stepmother to
Modesty; her matronly countenance bespeaks firmness.
The bristle of her brows and the sobriety of her thoughts
Give clear indication of her devout disposition.   20
No smile on her face sighs for the ways of Venus.
Nor does she hint at wantonness by any loose word.
The power of Marcia's character makes vice a captive
And transforms the weaker sex into the stronger.
Wantonness falsifies sex just as the nutshell,   25
So harmful to the teeth, hides the succulent kernel.
Breaking a jar would show how strong it is and
The scent of honey would abound within the yew bark.
The yew yield honey and the hemlock smell of honey,
Were a firm faith to flourish in a frail breast.   30
A marvel—winter blossoms with spring flowers, the crow
Turns white; vinegar smacks of nectar, the yew of honey,
The myrrh of roses. Marcia glorifies womanhood, dignifies
Human nature; she makes the yew a honey-bearer,
She checks inborn baseness; but no aversion to   35
Chaste love banishes the spiritual glory of it.
The sweetness of the nut contends with the nutshell, and
The unsightly honeycomb wars with the flavor within.
Marcia, frank, devoted, chaste, and decorous, is aghast
At adulterating sexuality with opposing goods.   40
As a patient warder she makes moral values firm;

She is the nurse of manners, the delightful companion of virtue.
In her lifetime Marcia deserved to be acknowledged as
Just by the just, holy by the holy, worthy of Cato by Cato.

56. Helen's radiant beauty of face and form—hers by
Nature's gift—needs no embellishment by artifice.
Her countenance puts to shame ordinary mortal form;
Beauty beyond beauty, she shines with the grace of stars.
Such beauty, knowing no peer, despised by inferiors,   5
Can rightly lay claim to the praises of the jealous.
Her golden hair, unfettered by any confining knot,
Cascades quite freely about her face, letting
The radiant beauty of her shoulders reveal
Their charms; its disarray pleases all the more.   10
Her brow shows its charms like words on a page;
Her face has no spot, no blemish, no stain.
Her dark eyebrows, neatly lined twin arches,
Set off skin that is like the Milky Way.
Her sparkling eyes rival the radiance of the stars,   15
And with engaging frankness play ambassadors of Venus.
With equal candor a blush that would make the captive
Rose pay tribute suffuses her face. As it fades away,
The blush proves no enemy to her face as rosy hue and
Snow-white skin contend in most delightful combat.   20
The line of her nose is not too boldly flat,
Nor is her nose set at too pert an angle.
The glory of that countenance is her rosy lips
Sighing for a lover's kiss, delicate lips
That break into laughter as delicate as they.   25
Lest ever they protrude in an unpleasant manner,
Those honied lips redden in laughter most delicate.
Her teeth are straight and even, and their whiteness
Like ivory. Her smooth neck and shoulders whiter than
Snow give way to firm but dainty breasts.   30

57. If one is fastidious, saying that there is no point to wordiness, let
him study this physical description:

Her teeth are like ivory, her broad forehead like milk,
Her neck snow, her eyes stars, her lips roses.
Her chest and waist are narrow and compact, giving
Way at last to the swell of her rounded abdomen.
Next is the area celebrated as the storehouse   5
Of modesty, the mistress of Nature, the delightful
Dwelling of Venus. Of that sweetness which lies
Hidden there, he that partakes can be the judge.
Neither the shapely leg, nor the trim knee, nor
The small foot, nor the smooth hand hangs with loose   10
Skin. Her appearance lacks no perfection;
She weds gracefulness of manner to Nature's dower.
The comeliness of her features, her exquisite form

Give her the appearance of a matchless beauty.
One is unable to say which is the more charming,   15
The sweetness of the parts or the perfection
Of the whole. But yet no winds of haughtiness bend
This prized flower; she is truly a rose without thorns.
This description is dedicated to Venus. I have chosen
For myself such things as Matthew loves to describe.   20
For this prize, Spartan bands laid waste Phrygian lands,
Looted Priam's realms, burned Troy, ruined powerful princes.
If Greece asks, "Why did Priam's son carry her off to Troy?",
Say, "Put Hippolytus alongside her and he will become
    Priapus."[16]

58. Beroe is a mangy cur, a pallid social outcast,
Horrid in appearance, the work of a Nature gone mad.
She is another Tesiphone, a public disgrace.
A mere specter, she is weighed down with wasting away.
Her body is filthy to look at and repulsive to touch.   5
Her itching neck denies her hand any rest.
The itch covers her head like a close-fitting cap,
And flies complain they find not a scrap of food.
Her head is bald and her parched skin like rust.
Dirt flows down her menacing brow—pale and unsightly.   10
Bushy brows bristling above bleary eyes make the upper
Half of her face a thicket of grime and filth.
Her eyebrows reaching down to cover her nose
Vainly try to offset a thin and wasted neck.
Her ears are packed with dirt; only the eyes   15
Do not seem to teem with worms. From them slime drips.
Her pale eyes have bloody matter running from them.
As soon as her bleary eyes seem dry of filth,
They fill up again and about her buzz hungry flies
Which her eyelids like mousetraps imprison in little baskets   20
Of foul matter. Her fetid flat nose that lies along
Her face at a distorted angle drips pestilential mucus.
This flow keeps her upper lip wet as the thick froth
From her nose returns to its diseased host.
Beroe's wretched cheeks are stiff and cracked with wrinkles;   25
In this forest of wrinkles one can spot her eyes by
The rheumy sickness welling up in them. Her drooping
Lips grow pale as her Stygian saliva manures her mouth's
Curving lines. A film covers her teeth, which are
Doubly destroyed by her stinking breath and by worms.   30
Her scabbiness extends down that repulsive mass of knots,
Sores, and streaming corruption called a neck. Enlarged veins
Draw and crisscross her chest, while the flabby skin
Of her breasts makes them look like deflated bladders.
She is nothing but skin and bones.   35
Her stomach swells out with sores which
The nearby Lethe, the doorway to her lower regions,
Stirs up. Oh wretched chaos of a woman! Even her

Height is contracted by a dreadful hump which,
To speak briefly, makes her back puff out.　　　　　40
Her chamber pot bristling with worn-out hairs is
A turbulent lake, and the waters of that sulphurous whirlpool
Run red. To gaze on her body is horrible—there
The underworld lies hidden, a lake brimming with filth.
The joints of her knees are stiff, yet　　　　　45
They are steeped in a painful flow of burning pus.
Her mangy shins are worm-eaten, and her gouty feet so
Painful that each toe suffers as though it were a foot.

59. The foregoing descriptions obviously are not all of the same type. Five commend their subjects, and two disparage them. There is less need, moreover, for instruction in vituperation, since the general tendency of human frailty inclines man to faultfinding.

60. Listeners, furthermore, should try to bear firmly in mind that in the descriptions given above they are to understand the general techniques of descriptions by means of examples involving specific persons; otherwise their understanding of the material will not be what the writer intends. Listeners should concentrate, not on what is said, but on the manner in which it is said. Therefore, those characteristics which are attributed to the Pope, or to Caesar, or to various persons who are described should be understood, not as peculiar characteristics of those particular persons, but as characteristics that may apply to other persons of the same social status, age, rank, office, or sex. Names of specific persons are thus used to represent a general class of persons and not to indicate special qualities belonging alone to those persons who are named. **61.** So Ovid writes:

I shall be called the Typhis and the Automedon of Love. (*Ars*, I, 6)

Or Virgil:

If any little Aeneas might play for me in my hall. (*Aen.*, IV, 328)

In these cases the proper names certainly stand for a general class. **62.** And so these epithets which apply to specific persons are to be interpreted as symbols of a class. Thus proper to the Pope is the power of binding and loosing; thus proper to Caesar is the desire to forge a way into forbidden territory and the longing for conflict which he vowed to make his way of life. As Lucan says:

He would rather burst a city gate than find it open to him. (*Phars.*,
　II, 443)

The same is true for the rest of the persons described.

63. In each description, moreover, many qualities ought to be set forth. For no one is sufficiently described by one or two or even just a few epithets. Just as a single rose does not show off very well when it is choked by many thorns or a single pearl glisten when it is buried in a marsh, so a person's worth is not sufficiently proclaimed by ascribing to him a single or even a few good points, when perhaps a host of vices may outweigh the scanty praise thus given. Therefore each person who is praised ought to be commended for a number of virtues, "for things that have little power taken singly please greatly when joined together" (Ovid, *Rem.*, 420).

64. Furthermore, if one is praising people, some epithets ought to be restricted to certain types of persons, some ought to be attributed to a fair number of persons, others ought to be attributed to all praiseworthy persons generally.

65. For example, in describing the pastor of a church, one ought to stress his steadfast faith, his longing for virtue, his religious devotion, his sweet words of compassion; his justice ought not to be enlarged upon, since too much emphasis on the pastor's rigorous justice might make him appear a tyrant. Here is the proper epithet for a pastor:

> He raises up the downtrodden and puts down the haughty. (Virg., *Aen.*, VI, 853)

66. On the other hand, a rigorous justice ought to be ascribed amply to a prince or emperor; if even a little wavering of his sense of justice is suggested, it would be to his detriment. For as Lucan says:

> If a man would be tender, let him depart from court. (*Phars.*, VIII, 494)

Nor was it superfluous to say earlier of Caesar:

> his skills are not exiled
> Nor does zeal drive out his imperial discipline. (I, 51, 25)

Indeed, I have read that someone made this notable distich about the idols at Rome which were replacing the gods as objects of devotion:

> To be a god is nonsense if your substance is stone
> And if your form comes from the hand of man.

67. Furthermore, in praising a woman one should stress heavily her physical beauty. This is not the proper way to praise a man. As Ovid says:

> A nonchalance over physical beauty is becoming in man. (*Ars*, I, 509)

In another place he puts it this way:

> A true man is concerned with his appearance
> Only within very moderate limits. (*Her.*, IV, 76)

68. Of course, sometimes a poet, to strengthen his case, describes the splendor of a young man's beauty as Statius did in his *Thebaid,* where he described the handsome Parthenopaeus as the very mirror of beauty. Statius emphasized this youth's beauty so that the reader might more easily understand the deep grief that even his enemies felt at his death. Statius calls him:

> The Arcadian whom both armies wept over equally. (*Theb.,* XII, 807)

Beauty, indeed, is the elegant and harmonious proportion of parts, accompanied by charming color. **69.** Also, one ought to attribute to a wife rigorous strictness, avoidance of sauciness, and shunning of incontinence and lust. Lust is, moreover, a vile and base business, which stems from the excitement of vile and base passions whose hunger is full of anxiety and whose satisfaction is full of sorrow. **70.** Similarly, other qualities ought to be assigned in a variety of ways to other persons, always in keeping with Horace's dictum:

> Let each style be employed only where it is fitting. (*Poet.,* 92)

71. There are other qualities which ought to be attributed to any man who is praised, such as that stern manliness which maintains itself in adversity as well as in prosperity; for the true man is one who prepares himself beforehand to face fortune's double offerings with a resolute singleness of mind and also with patience, which is the preserver of virtue. As Prudentius says:

> It is a widowed virtue that does not
> Have patience as its protector. (*Psych.,* V, 177)

Or Cato:

> Of all habits, the most excellent is patience. (*Dist.,* I, 38)

72. In the foregoing descriptions, moreover, if two or more verses have the same meaning, it should be understood that these were not written frivolously but were deliberately planned to avoid imputing a fault by not mentioning a virtue and also to mention all virtues necessary to offset a possible fault.

73. Since the exercise of the craft of versification consists especially in skill in description, I would advise that if a thing is described, the greatest attention be paid to credibility in writing descriptions, so that what is said either is true or seems to be true. This practice agrees with Horace's advice:

> Either follow tradition or invent
> Details that agree with each other. (*Poet.,* 119)

Thus Lucan describes Curio in the following way because he was thus easily able to make clear Curio's desire for a civil war:

> Joining them was Curio, a reckless man with a venal tongue.
> He had once been the voice of the people
> And a defender of freedom who had even dared to reduce
> Armed chieftains to the level of the common people. (*Phars.*, I, 269)

Similarly, he describes Cato, who did not hesitate to choose suicide rather than be reduced to servitude to Caesar and have to beg from him a reward for his virtue:

> He was husband and father to the whole city;
> A worshipper of justice, a strict observer of honor;
> He was a good man for the commonwealth. (*Phars.*, II, 388)

74. One should, moreover, note that a twofold description of any person is possible: one external, one internal. The external describes bodily graces; that is, it focuses on the exterior man. The internal describes the qualities of the inner man such as reason, faithfulness, patience, honesty, double-dealing, arrogance, or prodigality and other characteristics of the inner mind, that is, of the spirit, which are set forth either for praise or censure.

75. Also in any description of a person, whether it is based upon office, sex, character, rank, or condition of life, one's general appearance ought to be fully delineated. Because the diversity of terms for the same meaning should not be allowed to block the reader's understanding, one must realize that "rhetorical colors," "epithet," "peculiar quality," and "personal attribute" all mean the same thing. The "peculiar quality" of any person consists in "personal attributes." For the sake of greater clarity in this work, I shall run briefly through these attributes by way of summary so that the careful listeners can more clearly develop in their own verses a point or an argument about a person or a thing on the basis of attributes. **76.** Of course, these terms "argument" or "point drawn from name or nature" are to be understood here in a sense different from their meaning in logic. For there is no such thing as an argument or point drawn from name or nature except through interpreting a name to praise or condemn a person or through showing that one's natural endowments are appropriate or inappropriate to his character.

77. There are, therefore, eleven personal attributes: name, nature, way of life, fortune, character, goals, appetites, judgment, luck, exploits, and eloquence.

78. A theme or point drawn from a name is a matter of interpreting a person's name to suggest something good or bad about the person, as Ovid does:

Maximus, you fill out the measure of a mighty name,
Doubling nobility of birth by that of soul. (*Pont.*, I, 2, 2)

Or to take a home-grown example, it is possible for a theme or point to
be made from a name as I did above in the description of Caesar:

Slayer Caesar lives up to his name; his slaying
Hand makes clear the significance of his name. (I, 51, 31)

79. We turn now to that attribute called nature. Tully divides this
into two classes,[17] mental attributes and physical attributes (*De inventione*, I, 24). **80.** An example of a physical attribute is seen in Statius's
description of Polynices:

That one quicker in pace and towering in stature. (*Theb.*, I, 414)

81. Or a mental attribute is seen in his description of Tydeus:

Tydeus was no less strong and spirited; for though his
Frame was smaller, greater courage reigned in every part. (*Theb.*,
I, 416)

82. Those attributes which are a result of nationality, native land,
age, family, or sex are extrinsic. A difference exists, moreover, between nationality and native land, for nationality refers to language
and native land to place of birth. Here, from Virgil, is a point based
upon nationality:

I fear the Greeks even when they come bearing gifts. (*Aen.*, II, 49)

In Statius we find a point based upon family ties:

Cadmus was the father of my fathers. (*Theb.*, I, 680)

And upon native land:

My land is Mavortian Thebes. (*Theb.*, I, 680)

And upon age in Ovid:

Can you believe that she was returned a virgin
By one both youthful and hot-blooded? (*Her.*, V, 129)

And upon sex in Virgil:

Away, come break off your delay;
Woman is always fickle and inconstant. (*Aen.*, IV, 569)

And in Juvenal:

A prodigal woman is never aware of her dwindling funds. (*Sat.*, VI,
362)

This is an argument from nature where it uses the word "woman."
Here is a single example that includes a number of descriptions:

Adrastus, though of modest stature, thrives on his
Native intelligence, having the air of a hero
Because of the distinction of his mind.

The argument is from nature—partly from the mind, where it says
"native intelligence" and partly from the body "of modest stature." It
is an argument from sex in the words "having the air of a hero because
of the distinction of his mind"; indeed, the word "hero" indicates age,
strength, sex, and status. Here is an argument from nationality:

Through evil the people of Gabo turned as sour as vinegar,
As the bitter disorder of their minds engulfed them in vice.

Here is an argument from native land:

Rome thirsts for gold, Rome loves those who give gold,
And Rome refuses to defend the accused from the giver.[18]

Or from family ties:

Etiocles, cursed child, repeats the evil of Oedipus,
Catching from his father a thirst for wickedness.

Or from age:

Love is a delightful friend for a fuzzy-cheeked youth;
For a graybeard, Venus is a ridiculous companion.

83. We turn now to an attribute derived from way of life. Thus, in
Lucan, Caesar is made to say of Pompey:

He was accustomed to lick the sword of Sulla. (*Phars.*, I, 330)[19]

Or, in Statius, Etiocles says, speaking of Argia:

Will your queen, accustomed to her father's luxury,
Endure this simple home? (*Theb.*, II, 438)

And, similarly, above I said of Davus:

He is so habituated to vice that he finds it hard
To break the habit, so he goes his habitual evil way. (I, 53, 25)

Also, this attribute is divided into one's customary food and table manners.

84. We turn now to fortune, another attribute which may serve as
the basis for a description. There are numerous examples. Juvenal
writes:

Nothing is more intolerable than a rich woman. (*Sat.*, VI, 461)

The argument is based on fortune because he says "rich." Ovid
says:

> Utmost misery is safe, for there is no fear of worse outcome.
> (*Pont.,* II, 2, 31)

Juvenal says:

> The empty-handed traveler will whistle in the robber's face. (*Sat.,*
> X, 22)

Horace says:

> Is rare speech ever found garbed in shabby dress?[20]

Statius says:

> It is pleasant for the unhappy to speak and recall old sorrows.
> (*Theb.,* V, 48)

For the state of being utterly overcome by misery, the safety of being able to whistle in the face of a robber, the gift of speaking rare truths, the pleasure that the afflicted find in past woes—all these touch on fortune. So does what I said earlier about Davus:

> His wickedness shows him a slave to madness. (I, 53, 81)

85. We turn now to descriptions based on character, examples of which are easily found. Ovid writes:

> He was not elegant Ulysses, but eloquent Ulysses. (*Ars,* II, 123)

Or to take another example from Ovid:

> Typhis was master of the Hemonian ship. (*Ars,* I, 6)

Since to say that someone is eloquent, masterful, honest, or artful indicates a lasting property of mind, these descriptions are based upon character. My earlier description of Ulysses illustrates this fact:

> This man from Ithaca
> Ranks first in genius; strong in mind, prudent in word,
> Mighty in cunning, he is ever mindful of honesty. (I, 52, 4)

"First in genius" is an argument from nature; "mindful of honesty" is based upon character; "strong in mind" is based upon nature, "prudent in word" upon eloquence, and "mighty in cunning" upon character. And in like manner it is possible in a different set of verses to find other personal attributes assigned to persons.

86. We turn now to that attribute called goals. A goal is any undertaking to which one willingly and ardently applies his mind. Statius shows us that goals may be used as the basis of a description:

> They are eager to exchange life for praise.[21]

We find this attribute also used by Horace:

> A man's goals change with age, his heart desires wealth
> And friends, and he becomes a slave to public acclaim. (*Poet.*, 166)

Horace uses this same attribute in his description of Vulteius Mena:

> He pines away over his goals and
> Grows old with his love of getting. (*Ep.*, I, 7, 85)

We can see this same thing in my description of Caesar above:

> He sighs
> For soldierly duties. (I, 51, 7)

87. We turn now to feeling, which is a sudden and passing change in either mind or body. This characteristic can serve as the basis of a description, as in Ovid:

> How hard it is for the guilty man
> Not to be given away by his looks. (*Met.*, II, 447)

Or again in Ovid:

> Besides all this, pleasant faces were at the table. (*Met.*, VIII, 677)

Or we can see it in the *Achilleid* of Statius:

> Oh, how joy adds greatly to beauty. (*Ach.*, I, 167)

Lucan affords another example:

> The idle crowd trembled at his fierce threats. (*Phars.*, V, 364)

Similarly, one could say of a timid maiden and a boy:

> Grave apprehension drove the roses from her cheeks
> And made their pallor illegal heir of fleeing color.

Here is another example:

> A blush is the interpreter of the mind and the prophet of
> Intent; it is a good guess that there is mischief afoot.

Clearly joy, fear, pallor, and other matters of outward appearance all pertain to feeling.

88. We turn now to that attribute called judgment. Judgment is the balanced weighing of an action in the scales of justice and reason. It is a careful sorting out of which alternatives to reject and which to choose. This quality can be used as the basis of description, as Lucan does when he makes Brutus say to Cato:

> Bolster my wavering heart, and let your
> Resolute strength correct my vacillation. (*Phars.*, II, 244)

This is as if he had said, "You are able to give steady judgment to me wavering between alternatives." Other examples are Statius's account of Adrastus's words:

> Our grief shall not blot out our judgment. (*Theb.*, III, 393)

Or in Claudian:

> Let regard for duty guide your mind. (Claud., VIII, 268 [*Honor.*])

Or also in my description of Ulysses:

> Not until he has weighed the rightness of a deed
> Does his hand, the friend of his mind's deliberation, act. (I, 52, 37)

89. We turn now to luck, which is the usual issue of adversity through which we can see something of men's characters. Thus we find in Lucan:

> The bands of Ilium with their usual bad luck
> Seek the standards of the camp doomed to fall. (*Phars.*, III, 211)

Here, "with their usual bad luck" refers, of course, to those Trojans who had earlier battled the Greeks and suffered a similar misfortune in the fall of Troy. Elsewhere Lucan writes:

> Fortune spares many that are guilty,
> And only with the lucky can the gods be angry. (*Phars.*, III, 448)

Or we may quote Statius where Argia pleads with Adrastus:

> Agree to war, Father; look on the low estate of your
> Fallen son-in-law. Father, see here the exile's child. (*Theb.*, III, 696)

Or Ovid:

> Ill-gotten gains beget no good fortune. (*Am.*, I, 10, 48)

Or we may use a home-made example:

> Only with difficulty does the wretched man arise
> Under the weight of his burden, only with difficulty
> Does he find joys in a life in which he is buffeted
> By the wintry winds of an angry fortune.

90. One must distinguish between fortune and luck. Luck is the outcome of any mishap that might afflict someone. Fortune, on the other hand, is a state in life at which a person has arrived either through his own efforts, the course of events, or the gift of someone else. Here are some examples: fortune through one's own efforts is someone's voluntarily assuming the hardships of poverty so that at some later date he may acquire gain; fortune through the course of events is someone's being defeated in battle and falling into poverty as a result of this defeat or, on the other hand, a victor's gaining some prerogative. Fortune through the gift of another is someone's being born heir to a king or other royal person. In this last circumstance we have an instance, not of nature, but of human institutions. So there is clearly a difference between fortune and luck because luck is transitory while fortune is, generally speaking, longer lasting and of greater effect.

91. We turn now to exploits which are customary practices from which something about a person may be inferred. Lucan affords an example when he has Caesar say:

> My exploits are enough; I have conquered the northern peoples;
> I have overcome hostile armies by fear alone. (*Phars.*, V, 660)

Or again we find in Lucan another example in his description of Caesar:

> Caesar, furious for war, rejoices
> To find no way except by bloodshed. (*Phars.*, II, 439)

My own earlier description of Caesar gives another example:

> Caesar's steadfastness shines in battle; he brooks
> No opposition; he breaks the brave; he tames the fierce. (I, 51, 1)

92. We turn now to language. Language is a customary way of speaking which reveals something about a person. An example of language as a personal attribute is found in Lucan's description of Caesar:

> Thus he spoke, unable to learn the language of a private
> Man even when he wore plebeian garb. (*Phars.*, V, 539)

Language is referred to in Horace:

> Not one idle word sticks in a wise man's mind. (*Poet.*, 337)

And in Ovid, speaking of Ulysses:

> His speech wanted no grace of manner. (*Met.*, XIII, 127)

Similarly, I said this of the Pope in my description of him:

> The Pope teaches what ought to be taught, prohibits what
> Ought to be prohibited, and condemns sin. He holds spiritual
> Sway. (I, 50, 13)

93. We turn now to the description of an action by its attributes. An action is something done or spoken on the basis of which some man or some woman may, as it were, be accused of infamous behavior; that is, the person is condemned on the basis of the charge which is lodged against him. **94.** There are nine attributes of an action; the gist of the action, the cause of the action, the action preceding the action described, the action accompanying the said action, the action following the said action, the ease with which it was done, the quality of the action, the time, and the place.

95. The gist of the action is what Tully calls "a short summary of the whole matter" (*De inventione,* I, 26). It is the name or the definition of the action itself. This is made the basis for a description in Juvenal:

> Who will not confound heaven with earth, and sea
> With sky if Verres denounces thieves or Milo cutthroats? (*Sat.,* II,
> 25)

Or in Lucan, describing Caesar speaking to his troops:

> You conquerors of the world on whom my fortune hangs. (*Phars.,*
> VII, 250)

Or in my earlier description of Davus:

> A roaming buffoon, a gluttonous parasite, an offscouring of
> The masses, Davus is a sickening pest, disgraceful in his deeds. (I,
> 53, 1)

96. We turn now to cause, which is divided into two kinds. One kind is impulsive, the other rational and logical. **97.** A cause is impulsive when we are precipitated into some action by a transitory feeling. Ovid illustrates this:

> Love made her bold. (*Met.,* IV, 96)

Or Juvenal:

> Told it's there, a hungry Greek will seek pie in the sky. (*Sat.,* III,
> 78)

A person who is driven by either love or hunger acts impulsively. The same is true about Jupiter and Ino, when he was forced to give the cow to Juno to relieve her suspicions:

> He gives the calf; he does not give it; he is forced to.
> Indeed, his surrendering the calf was like the maiden's
> Surrendering her honor; neither gave willingly.

98. A rational or logical cause is evident when one chooses what is advantageous or shuns what is disadvantageous. Lucan affords an example of a description based upon choosing the advantageous:

> Meanwhile Magnus, unaware of the chief's capture, was readying his
> Troops so that by a show of strength he might firm up his
> forces. (*Phars.,* II, 526)

Or Horace:

> I shall strive for a poetic style created from the familiar language
> So that anyone may think that he can write this way. (*Poet.*, 240)

Lucan also illustrates the shunning of the disadvantageous:

> Then Caesar, fearing that his front line might be shaken
> By their first wave, held some cohorts in reserve
> Behind his standard and at an angle to his front line. (*Phars.*, VII,
> 521)

As does Horace:

> Lest by chance I assign a youth the traits
> Of an old man or a boy that of a man, I shall
> Always take care that one's traits fit his age. (*Poet.*, 176)

Similarly, it is possible to base a description upon a rational motive that involves choosing the advantageous and shunning the disadvantageous:

> The lover can possess his beloved and not let love
> Cool, if he pursues her with entreaties or gifts.

An example of shunning the disadvantageous is in "and not let love cool" and of choosing the advantageous in "the lover can possess his beloved." But it may seem that a rational cause is the same as judgment and that therefore an attribute based upon cause is really a personal attribute instead of an attribute of a thing. **99.** But this is not so; for judgment refers to the judgment of the person, not to the judgment of the thing. The cause, on the other hand, is the cause of the thing, not the cause of the person.

100. We turn now to attributes based upon the action which precedes that action being described, is concomitant with the matter being described, or follows the matter being described. These attributes are the circumstances of the main action; that is, they are the things that precede, accompany, or follow the main action that serves as the basis of a description. **101.** A description can be based upon those things which precede the main action, as in Lucan:

> Blood had already touched the defiled swords of Caesar. (*Phars.*,
> II, 536)

102. Or upon those things which accompany it; again I cite Lucan:

> The fury of Gaul is pouring over the snowy Alps. (*Phars.*, II, 535)

Or upon those things which follow the main action. Again I cite Lucan:

> What lands will be given my veterans to plough, what
> Walls will shelter the disabled ones? (*Phars.*, I, 344)

Or I can refer to Juvenal:

> When one has put on the war helmet,
> It is too late to regret battle. (*Sat.,* I, 169)

I can offer an example of my own which illustrates all three of these attributes:

> Gladly welcomed love-play, union, pregnancy—
> These are the threefold sign of virginity's loss.

103. The description is based upon what precedes the action when the verse says, "gladly welcomed love-play," for the consent of the mind is the precursor of amorous pleasure. The description is based upon what accompanies the action when the verse says "union." And, of course, the description is based upon what follows the action when the verse says "pregnancy."

104. We turn now to the ease with which the deed is done. This attribute is considered only briefly; it is illustrated in Ovid:

> To deceive a trusting maid is not a hard-won glory. (*Her.,* II, 63)

Or in:

> It is easy for the simple mind to be deceived into deceiving,
> For simplicity with its ready credulity is easily misled.

105. We turn now to the mode or quality of the action. Horace speaking of Homer affords us an example:

> He invents so carefully, intermingling fiction with fact
> That the beginning does not disagree with the middle,
> Nor the middle with the end. (*Poet.,* 151)

Also Virgil in his *Eclogues:*

> Was he not to hand over to me, a victor over him in singing,
> A goat which my pipe won by its songs? (*Ecl.,* III, 21)

Or Lucan:

> Why do you keep away the world's swords from Caesar's blood?
> (*Phars.,* VII, 81)

Similarly, it is possible to write:

> A too easy belief is hurtful,
> A quick hand usually does a regrettable job. (Matt., *Pyr. and Th.,* 125)

In Ovid we find:

> Every impulse suggests a difficult course of action. (*Rem.,* 120)

106. We turn now to a description based upon the time of the action. A description may be based upon time if one is able to conjecture something either good or bad about the action on the basis of the suitability of the time. As in Virgil's *Bucolics:*

> Now all things are in bloom, now is the year loveliest. (*Ecl.,* III, 57)

107. Similarly, one could take my own example in which the four seasons of the year are described, under the restraint of brevity, in this way:

Description of the Four Seasons

> Rosy springtime runs riot with delicate flowers,
> The very earth labors to wreathe Rhea's hair with flowers.
> Then the friendly warmth of the sun grows warmer
> As the sun proves himself king of the summer.
> Autumn, the vintner, the cupbearer of Bacchus, pours forth   5
> The sweetness of grapes and fills the barns with ample harvest.
> Bound with three layers of clothes, winter stiffens with cold;
> This stepmother of flowers is a sorry companion to a sportive
>   mood.

108. Here are epithets of the four seasons set forth in abbreviated form. The four seasons are described as two pairs:

> Spring grows warm, but the summer grows hot;
> Autumn gives wine, but the winter freezes it.

Or thus:

> Spring is the parent of flowers, summer the nurse of harvest,
> Autumn the vintner, and then comes prodigal winter.
> Venus, harbinger of the sun's rising, puts stars to flight,
> And a better day dawns at night's retreat.
> Aurora binds the night in exile, and Tithonus   5
> Leaving his couch makes ruddy the face of Jove.
> Light accompanied by a prickly cold creeps across the sky
> As the gray dawn strives to become full-blown day.
> Now Phoebus sends forth his beams more fully;
> His chargers pant along their course seeking the midday mark.   10
> Now his chariot descends toward the Antipodes, his wheels
> Ever farther, ever more slowly sinking down into the West.

109. We turn now to a description based upon place. A description may be based upon place when the aptness of the location allows one to conjecture that something was or was not done. We see this in Horace:

> Gracious Athens added more of knowledge (*Ep.,* II, 2, 43)

Or in Lucan:

> Curio was joyous as though the luck of the place
> Itself should wage the war. (*Phars.*, IV, 661)

110. Since descriptions should not be needlessly multiplied, one ought to note that a description based upon time or place may be often superfluous, often apt. Unless we suggest something of importance to our listeners by details of time and place which we wrap around our account, these details ought to be omitted. An example of the apt use of description of a place is seen in Cicero's oration against Verres.[22] When Cicero refuted Verres's defense against the charge of corruption in Sicily, he described the many attractions of that country. He spoke of trees renowned for the goodness of their fruit, of blooming meadows as pictures of living beauty, of clear springs bubbling with pure water, so that when his readers understood the loveliness of the country, they would consider Verres, who committed adultery in the midst of such great beauty, to have even more unbridled lusts than Cicero had imputed to him. **111.** One might describe a place along the lines of this topographical description of mine:

Description of a Place

This spot is nature's rarest triumph; here abound
The charms, the delights, the riches of spring.
Nature fawns over this place, so generously giving it
Every favor that can be bestowed that nothing is lacking.
Exceeding the measure of that which has to be given,   5
Nature keeps nothing back for herself as she adorns this place
With flowery charm. The earth luxuriates with spikey herb.[23]
But brevity, the friend of the ear, pleases as it compresses.
The heat of the sun never reaches its waters,
As leafy fronds of sheltering boughs keep the water cool.   10
Moisture joining its power to the gentle rays of the sun
Makes all spring forth in flowery splendor.
Still another of Nature's gifts is the birds
Whose ardent chirping crowns the beauty of the place.
Crying out, "I perish," the sad nightingale sings[24]   15
And bemoans her plight with melodious plaint.
Now there sounds forth the song of the wild blackbird,
Which when tamed is usually renowned for his harsh cry.
Now the parrot, a fit exhibit for Caesar's triumph,
Exclaims in a tongue not its own, "Farewell."   20
Next Tereus appears armed for crime or for conflict.[25]
The gladsome lark with prophet's voice signals daybreak.
The proud peacock glittering with the hundred eyes of Argus
Rejoices in the splendor of his plumage. The dove
Sacred to Venus builds a nest among a tree's branches,   25
Wreathing its incestuous home with the simplest of leaves.

The faithful turtledove widowed of its mate groans,
Desirous of having continued its plighted love.
Here live and sing the distinctly spotted quail
And the partridge destined for the torment of the spit.   30
Across the clear water resounds the swan who, disdaining
The moment of death, sings its own funeral song.
The magpie cloaks itself in ambiguous colors
That give rise to disputes among logicians.
Here is a dwarf kingbird, who ennobles his   35
Short stature by the dignity of his name. The builder
Woodpecker, whose artful beak chisels out a covered home,
Now for himself, now for his kin, is not absent.
The chattering and greedy jackdaw, accustomed
To honoring exiled Lares, lurks in deep shade.   40
The sparrow, whose very name shows his spare
Satisfaction of the passion surging in his loins,
Either suffers or mates. No crow, no raven, no owl
Blasphemes this sacred place with harsh cries.
Here no eagle holds sway; no distinctions of rank   45
Trouble the songs of the multitude. Thus when
Each bird voices its complaint in moving notes, that song
Comes to the aid of the musician. Here blossoms bloom
Sweetly, herbs grow vigorously, trees leaf profusely.
Fruits abound, birds chatter, streams murmur, and   50
The gentle air warms all. Birds please with song, groves
With shade, breezes with warmth, springs with drink,
        streams with
Murmuring, the earth with flowers. Pleasant is the stream's
Sound, harmonious the birdsongs, sweet the flowers, cool
The springs, warm the shade. All five senses feast here,   55
As one may note by noticing all details described.
The stream appeals to the touch, the sweetness to the taste,
The birds to the ear, beauty to the eyes, and fragrance to the nose.
Not one of the four elements is wanting; the earth bears,
The air fosters, the heat quickens, the water nourishes.   60
The virgin makes flowing spring and charming flower,
The work of zealous Genius, favorable to herself.[26]

112. Some of the attributes of an action refer to its performance
and others concern merely the fact of the action. Among the latter attributes are the gist of the action, the cause of the action, and the
threefold matter of what occurred before the action, with it, and after
it. The performance of an action involves these other four attributes:
the quality of the action, the ease with which it was done, the time, and
the place. There are also two other kinds of attributes of an action,
matters collateral to an action and matters consequent upon an action.
But a discussion of these must be omitted for the moment lest prolix
explication burden reading with tedium and the reader with distaste.

113. Indeed, the necessary attributes of any action are time and
place, which are inseparable, for if any action exists, it must be at some

time and in some place. Time and place ought to be described at length. Thus critics must not jump on me because of the fullness of the preceding topographical description which, although it may have been executed with a heavy hand, has nevertheless been done as an original little work, "so that a little crow which has been stripped bare of its stolen colors can provoke laughter" (Hor., *Ep.,* I, 3, 19). For indeed, certain persons, who will remain nameless, glory "in living on crumbs from another man's table" (Juv., *Sat.,* V, 2) and have thus presumed to claim as their own these topographical verses.

114. Many examples, moreover, are no more superfluous for the attributes of an action than for the attributes of a person. If two or more examples are given, the first ought to be clear, the second clearer, the third clearest. Just as a building is stronger if its support comes from a diversity of columns, so a wealth of examples benefits a description. A mouse could easily be caught without a mousetrap if a single mousehole were its only refuge.

115. If, moreover, a diversity of attributes occurs in the same description, this is because description ought to have the effect of polished discourse, not merely of conversation. For words are to be understood on the basis of the sense in which they are used, not merely on the basis of the sense they make. This fact can be seen from a quotation I cited earlier:

> Can you believe that she was returned a virgin
> By one both youthful and hot-blooded? (I, 82)

Where the line says "youthful," we have an attribute based upon nature; where it says "hot-blooded," we have an attribute based upon disposition. And it is similar in many instances. Thus an example ought to focus the mind upon what is being exemplified. **116.** This little verse lists all the attributes of an action as well as those of a person:

> Who, what, where, with what aid, why, when, in what manner.

"Who" includes the eleven personal attributes; "what" includes the gist of the action and the threefold matter of what comes before, with, and after an action; "where" includes place; "with what aid" the ease of doing the action; "why" the cause, "when" the time; and "in what manner" includes the quality of the action.

117. Further, lest it seem that the principles taught in the foregoing descriptions are at odds with traditional teachings, I would point out that one can always use *zeugma* and *hypozeuxis* as well as other colors or figures. This will become clearer in following sections. In the preceding verses the listener should pay more attention to the method of speaking than to the substance of what was said, since in this little work gracefulness of expression is more important than the weightiness of what is expressed.

118. Moreover, lest longwindedness, from whose womb springs disgust, undertake to affront gracious ears, and so that "no man will be forced to accept my gift," for:

It is no less labor to have broken off speaking,

this section of my little work will be concluded forthwith. Also, the charm of a song repeated too often turns to revulsion in the ears of its listeners.

Lest the lyre turn sour, I rest. Delay is stepmother to
Acclaim. Part of my work remains; part is done.

These lines will serve as a transition:

Sicilian muses, let us sing songs a bit nobler, (Virg., *Ecl.,* IV, 1)
We hoist sails on seas made gracious by thy grace.
Neither orchards nor the humble tamarisks please all; (Virg.,
     Ecl., IV, 2)
At times only the laurel affords pleasure.

II

ELEGANCE OF WORDS

1. Since in the first part of this work I have spent some time discussing the writing of descriptions, I must now turn to the threefold elegance of versification. To charm my audience I have introduced a dream-vision imagined as having occurred the night before and worth relating to make them more receptive to learning by means of a pleasant story; to sharpen the attention, foster goodwill, encourage a desire to listen, avert boredom; and to whet the appetite for instruction. **2.** Indeed, in the early hours of the past night I seemed to see that as the bonds of wintry idleness were being broken, Flora, the doorkeeper of Spring, had adorned the bosom of the earth with a variegated mantle of flowers and had poured forth her gracious favor on the citadels of learning more than elsewhere, so the subtle sweetness of its scent might bring to those eager for wisdom both a respite from old labors and strength for new work. Or to put it more plainly, the face of the earth was so gaily decked and sweet fragrances grew so strong, having been taken by the vehicle of smelling to the domicile of reason, that whatever might doze there, lulled into a slumber by the dying coals of oblivion, my tongue can with the aid of a faithful memory set forth most pleasingly. Other gardeners lose sleep over the charms of the place I have described, as they work their artifices as though envious of zealous Flora. They turn a mediocrity barely acceptable into the equal flaw of an abundance almost wasteful. In the spot of which we are speaking it is indeed as if the flowers, to fulfill a vow made at birth, grow to maturity in their tender infancy. They think it unworthy to be held in their cradles and rise, not yet full-grown, to sport in merriments.

A Description of Nature

3. The guardian spirit of this spot strives to make it always
More beautiful; the spring covers earth's bosom with a grassy
Mantle. Each small plant thrives; a gentle breeze proclaims
Spring's gracious beauty. Flowers of every sort abound,
And the new-blown rose testifies to the mild air. A stream   5
Clear as glass nourishes fresh blossoms; this stream sweet

As nectar adds its fragrance to that of the flowers. Harsh
Numbing cold never spoils, never blasts the mild clime;
The flowers ever wear the appearance of the friend of spring.

A Description of Philosophy and Her Attendants

4. In this place of elegance that I have described, Lady Philosophy accompanied by a band of attendants retires from her toil to refresh her spirit amidst the fragrance of so many flowers. For her it is joy, now to lie among the flowers, now to wander among them.

5. Lady Philosophy is not painted with artificial charms but rather is seen clearly to produce an almost divine aura and to loathe any hint of the weakness of human nature. The dignified expression of her face shows a thoroughgoing modesty. Her stern brow gives no wanton nod as an invitation to looseness. The ardor of her eyes, gazing with straight and penetrating glance, scorns to look aslant. Her cheeks, unadulterated by false color, glow with the rosy hue of exercise. Her modest lips dwell closely together and are not frequently parted for idle words. Her face is beautified by that nobility which betokens the proper use of the mind. Her form is so graced with endless vigor that it belies natural frailty. Her stature cannot be described by such a fixed term as short or tall. Her garments, as Boethius says, are made of the finest threads, with the most subtle workmanship.[27] Their material is everlasting. Human ingenuity is too weak to set forth her disposition and her other attributes. She beggars all description. One must simply confess that to undertake such a description offends common sense. While Lady Philosophy speaks the gracious wisdom of her eloquent heart to her foster daughters and her other followers, striving to find examples to teach them by, Tragedy, shouting various loud cries in the midst of the group:

Throws out bombast and jawbreaker words. (Hor., *Poet.,* 97)

And relying on buskin feet, an inflexible appearance, and a menacing brow, Tragedy thunders forth a multitude of warnings, all with her customary ferocity.

6. On the side next to her sits Satire, fasting from silence; although her brow is filled with timidity, her downcast eyes give testimony to the slyness of her mind. Even her lips are widespread from constant chatter. She also makes a big show of her modesty which has never blushed at the naked body.

7. Now a third figure creeps forward slowly. It is Comedy, whose bowed head and workaday garb give no hint of merriment.

8. A fourth arises; it is:

Elegy who sings of quivered lovers. (Ovid, *Rem.,* 379)

She has a most pleasing brow, eyes almost provocative, and a pert expression. Her sweet lips seem to sigh for kisses. This last one comes forward haltingly, not because of any baseness of gait, but rather because of her unequal feet. Yet the effect of her pleasing stature makes up for any limping defect. She bears out Ovid's words:

> A defect in the feet will cause a graceful walk. (*Am.,* III, 1, 10)

Such are the four who hold sway in the realm of metrical verse, while they contend among themselves for the title "Queen of Poetry," for:

> There is little trust among metrical allies, and each is
> Unable to endure sharing authority with another.[28]

9. But I hear Elegy explaining the threefold elegance of versification, for there are three types of elegance which please in poetry: polished words (*verba polita*), figurative expression (*dicendi color*), and the inner sentiment (*interior favus*). This is to say that elegance in verse comes either from the beauty of its ideas, the exterior decoration of the words, or the quality of its speech.

10. Horace provides an example of the elegance which derives from the beauty of ideas:

> It is worthwhile to advance to a point
> Even if it is not in our power to go farther. (*Ep.,* I, 1, 32)

As does Lucan:

> When many err, the fault goes unpunished. (*Phars.,* V, 260)

In these examples the grace does not derive from any exterior verbal elegance, for the words are just those of ordinary speech. Nor does it come from the quality of the speech, for there are neither tropes nor other rhetorical figures. Rather it stems from the general ideas found in each example. Thus the beauty of what the words signify overflows to grace the very words themselves.

11. That grace of verses which comes from exterior verbal elegance is evident when the beauty of a verse is the result of felicitous expression which makes the reader regard the verse favorably, as in Lucan:

> Every honor lies hidden, dressed in plebeian garb. (*Phars.,* II, 18)

Or in the *Achilleid* of Statius:

> Day arising from Ocean dispels a world wrapped in dewy
> darkness. (*Ach.,* II, 1)

In regard to this point writers of verses must be set straight lest they produce only an ill-kempt assortment of words that seem to be beggars trying to relieve their poverty of ornament. To continue this metaphor drawn from material things, no one can fashion a gay costume from odds and ends of old rags; just as a bit of yeast ferments the entire mixture, so it is in verses. If there is going to be felicitous disposition of words, this felicity of diction must be reflected in the material itself. Otherwise, the lack of elegance in the verse will show either the ignorance or the negligence of the versifier. So just as the addition of a pearl or an emblem to a worthy garment will make the whole costume seem more elegant, there are some expressions—gems of diction— whose artful use makes the whole composition seem more felicitous. This type of ornamentation, moreover, for its part adds the advantages of its beauty to these other ways of speaking and reinforces their pleasant effects with its own elegance.

12. Since any good principle set forth for public use ought to enlighten one—a hidden lamp is of no use whatever—this work, therefore, will indicate those forms of expression which add to elegance. And, moreover, to inform youthful learners, I will give examples of their use. Certain of these words are adjectives formed from nouns and certain are adjectives formed from verbs. This, however, does not mean that nouns are wholly excluded from metrical elegance. But since the number of adjectives to be considered predominates, I give adjectives fuller treatment, nouns less. Nor is it meaningless to say verb-adjectives, for certain verbs are substantives, certain are vocatives, certain are adjectives.[29] But the elegance of language is most frequently found in noun-adjectives and verb-adjectives. This is true because there are certain proprieties in the use of these words, and elegance in versification consists in a scrupulous observation of these proprieties.

13. I will first discuss adjectives and what sort of combinations they demand in metrical versification. This will be done first by the example of verses and then by the example of phrases. These words, moreover, have various endings.

14. Some end in *-alis;* some in *-osus;* others in *-autus, -uus,* and *-aris.* There are, of course, other endings for adjectives. But by using examples, I can show how the felicitous joining of words can be most gracefully and elegantly done.

15. Some of these endings are less common than others; here are some words ending in *-alis: officialis, materialis, effigialis, venalis, superficialis, triumphalis, favoralis, exsequialis, mysterialis, imperialis, pontificalis, solstitialis, judicialis, initialis, conjecturalis, exitialis, prodigialis, legalis, connubialis,* and *collateralis.* [English equivalents used in this translation are these adjectives ending in *-al: official, material, artificial, venal, superficial, triumphal, general, funereal, universal, ceremonial, legal, imperial, pontifical, aestival, initial, conjectural, unnatural, mortal, connubial,* and *collateral.*] Here are some examples of how to use these words. (Some are to be followed, others to be avoided.)

> The sign of the pastor is his *official* flock.
> *Official* honors glorify the clergy.
> *Material* goods expand culture.

Or thus:

> *Artificial* glory is beauty's thief.
> *Artificial* glory can enrich things.

16. Here follows an example based upon the word *triumphal,* which seems to be a great favorite among unskilled writers whose presumptuous knowledge destroys discipline. These writers are like an unworthy hired hand who usurps the position of the shepherd, or like an unworthy dependent who tries to unseat his patron. It does not matter what sort of man these fellows present us with; it always seems as though a third Cato has fallen from heaven into our midst (Juv., *Sat.,* II, 40). Perhaps they "know how to picture a cypress" (Hor., *Poet.,* 19),[30] these frauds who raise a building without laying a foundation, who strive to work without any material. If I wished to give examples of this fault to help others, I certainly could; "my very wealth impoverishes me" (Ovid., *Met.,* II, 466). They disguise the blindness of thorough ignorance with the mask of superficial learning. **17.** Horace assails them, saying:

> You imitators, you slavish herd. (*Ep.,* I, 19, 19)

Then he compares them to the inept Iarbitas who, trying to imitate the oratorical prowess of Tymagenes with mere ranting declamation, burst his diaphragm. As Horace says:

> Iarbitas strove so hard to be considered
> Eloquent and polished that his very tongue
> Vying with Tymagenes caused him to burst asunder. (*Ep.,* I, 19,
> 15)

18. I will scoff at them through these examples:

> Syllables are *venal,* gems *superficial,* or medicine
> *Triumphal* in the mouths of wretched writers.

19. Furthermore:

> Fame delights the rabble with *general* acclaim.

Or thus:

> *General* popularity gives one a good name.

Further:

> The cry of the owl is a *funereal* sign of death.

Further:

> The words of a prophet have *universal* generality.

Or thus:

> Boxwood makes a *ceremonial* covering for a cross.   5

Or thus:

> The presbyter sings the *ceremonial* funeral ceremony.

Or thus:

> A citizen fears the *legal* judgment of a law court.

Or thus:

> *Imperial* Cupid governs even the gods. (Matt., *Pyr. and Th.,* 26)

Or thus:

> A *pontifical* hand wields the spiritual scepter.

Or thus:

> Pontiffs wield the *pontifical* scepter.   10

Further:

> Each summer produces *aestival* sorrows.

Further:

> The defendant shudders at the prospect of a *legal* trial.

Further:

> Eve was the *initial* seed of evil.

Or thus:

> Divine awe is the *initial* good.

(Because "fear of the Lord is the beginning of wisdom.") (Prov., 9:10)
Further, the ordinary mind speaks with expression and words:

> The prophet of doom exhibits *conjectural* signs in his face.   15

Here are some usages that may be taken as examples:

> An *unnatural* sin is a *mortal* evil.
> A *legal* compact, but *connubial* union.
> Love is the *collateral* defect of beauty.

20. The next section treats of adjectives ending in *-osus* [English examples in *-ous*]. Since Apella,[31] the credulous Jew, was convinced by examples drawn from real authors, some of the examples will be from older authors; some will be my own.

> Believe me, to give is *ingenuous.* (Ovid, *Am.,* I, 8, 62)

Or thus:

> Strength of spirit is an *ingenuous* comrade.

Or as Ovid says:

> The *courteous* Muse comes also to those unwilling to receive her. (*Pont.,* I, 120)

Or thus:

> The *courteous* hand serves the other members of the body.

Or as Claudian says:

> *Imperious* greed, the quarrelsome nursemaid of strife. (Claud., III, 30 [*Rufin.*]) 5

Or thus:

> *Imperious* splendor becomes a ruler.

Further:

> Even a *fastidious* love changes the appearances of things.

Or thus:

> A *fastidious* love impoverishes the richest vocabulary.

Or thus:

> A *fastidious* appetite scorns turnips.

Further:

> *Ambitious* greed torments the envious. 10

Further:

> An *ingenious* carefulness is quite discerning.

Further:

> Falling in love is an *impetuous* fault of adolescents.

Further:

> I have an *envious* thirst for excellence.

Further:

To trust a redheaded man is *monstrous*.

Further:

Superfluous verbosity covers up poetry.   15

Further:

Suspicious guesses pave the way for terror.

Further:

An *insidious* oracle causes one to lose faith.

Further:

A *contentious* tongue harms its owner.

Further:

Love between the aged is *ridiculous*.

21. The following treats of adjectives ending in *-atus*, such as *materiatus, orbiculatus, particulatus, articulatus, inveteratus, intemeratus, immediatus, immoderatus, insatiatus, inviolatus, irrevocatus*, and of participles of similar form, such as *intitulatus, primitiatus, intumulatus, illaqueatus, inviolatus, infiliatus, phaleratus*, and *enucleatus*. [English equivalents in this translation are these adjectives ending in *-ate: innate, orbiculate, aureate, ornate, articulate, inveterate, temperate, moderate, immoderate, insatiate, inviolate*, and *intemperate*, as well as participles of a similar form, such as *celebrated, created, unmated, captivated, violated, unabated, calculated*, and *unadulterated*.] Here are some examples of how these words may be used:

Skillful craftsmen increase the *innate* value of material things.

Further:

An *orbiculate* house is similar to the eye.

Further:

Aureate arguments win debates.
(For *ornate* truths persuade audiences.)

Further:

An *articulate* speaker gladdens his hearers.   5

Further:

An *inveterate* habit is hard to break.

Further:

A *temperate* father aids one.

Further:

Everyone enjoys a *moderate* clime.

Or one may illustrate adjectives through the use of phrases such as:

Immoderate love, *insatiate* hunger,
Inviolate trust, *intemperate* horde. 10

22. Participles with these endings can be considered along with adjectives having the same endings. Indeed a participle is both an adjective and a verb form. It is an adjective in terms of meaning and a verb form in terms of origin. Thus we have:

The *celebrated* king is sprung from noble ancestors.

Further:

From the spray of the sea came the newly *created* Venus.

Further:

When the law falters, duty remains *unmated.*

Further:

That man *captivated* by a maid must expect good and ill.

Or thus:

The man *captivated* by a maid fears nothing that he ought. 5

Further:

A maid not yet *violated* tortures the lustful.

Further:

A bad bite produces *unabated* suffering.

Further:

Deceit often lies hidden, *calculated* to mislead.

Further:

Unadulterated faithfulness thrives on service.

23. Other examples may be found that fit this pattern, such as *amplificatus, notificatus, vociferatus, continuatus,* and *certificatus.* But I must pass over many of these examples whose use in poetry is bandied about by barbers and drunks.[32] There is no point in discussing those

unrefined expressions whose use encumbers the poet so that he is like
Neoptolemus "who now for the first time comes as a soldier in new
arms" (Ovid, *Ars*, I, 36). The fewer details, moreover, that burden a
diligent listener, the more effective is the teaching. I repeat that when
one talks too much, what one says goes in one ear and out the other.
Therefore:

> When someone runs an idea into the ground, his teaching
> Is wasted; all teaching that wanders into repetition
> Sinks under the weight of this fault and is futile.

24. Next I will give some examples of adjectives ending in *-ivus*, such
as *relativus, vocativus, adoptivus, expositivus, responsivus, continuativus,
abusivus, incentivus, conjunctivus, collativus, effectivus, impulsivus,
negativus, redivivus,* and *petitivus.* [English equivalents in this translation are these adjectives ending in *-ive: relative, ineffective, active, adop-
tive, persuasive, meditative, tentative, abusive, incentive, seductive, collec-
tive, effective, compulsive, negative,* and *responsive.*] Here are some examples:

> True friendship rejoices in honors *relative* to one's merit. (Matt.,
> *Tob.,* 1414)

(For as Ovid says:

> The crowd tests friendship by mere utility.) (*Pont.,* II, 3, 8)

Or I might draw an example from the conversation of lovers about to
undergo the pangs of parting:

> In turn they postpone parting, crying in turn,
> "God speed, God speed," an *ineffective* way of preventing
> Tears from the one departing or the one remaining.

Further:

> A gentle brow bespeaks an *active* courtesy. (Matt., *Milo,* 18)

Further:

> Christ nurtures us with the kindness
> A father bestows upon an *adoptive* son.

5

Further:

> A *persuasive* hand may conceal a deceitful mind.

Or thus:

> A *persuasive* tongue is no deceiver.

(For the lips speak the thoughts of the heart.) Further:

> My verses are cast in a *meditative* mood.

Further:

> No love takes pleasure in a *tentative* liaison. 10

Further:

> Sacred public pronouncements avoid *abusive* statements.

Further:

> An *incentive* to evil darkens the face.

(Here, of course, *incentive* is a noun, not an adjective.) Further:

> A mistress hopes to prove a *seductive* companion.

Further:

> The prosecutor proved just the opposite; he assembled 15
> All the facts that pointed to *collective* sedition.

Further:

> An *effective* purpose marks a spiritual work.

(For the result of its purpose is that one must respond.) Further:

> A *compulsive* need makes a wicked act acceptable.

(For necessity knows no law.) Further:

> A *negative* reply makes desire even stronger.

(For according to Ovid:

> We always seek that which is forbidden
> And desire that which is denied. [*Am.*, III, 4, 17]

After this Ovid remarks:

> He to whom sin is permitted sins the least; the very
> Chance to sin makes the urges toward evil less compelling.) (*Am.*,
>   III, 4, 9)

Further:

> The prostitute is *responsive* to solicitation. 20

(Because we have Ovid's testimony:

> The only chaste woman is one whom no one has asked.) (*Am.*, I, 8,
>   43)

Or thus:

> When Thaïs is solicited, her *responsive* tones are eager.

25. There are, moreover, many words with these endings which are used only rarely, and thus they are not readily joined with the more important nouns. These words have lost their real meanings, so the fact that there are few examples of these adjectives is certainly understandable. Also, many words with these endings are not suitable to poetry because of their metrical quality and difficult syllabification, such as *indicativus, deprecativus,* and similar words.[33]

26. I will now discuss the few adjectives that end in *-aris,* such as *articularis, particularis, exemplaris, popularis,* and *famularis.* [English equivalents in this translation are *arthritic, specific, civic, paradigmatic,* and *sycophantic.*] Thus we have:

> *Arthritic* pains attack the joints (as in gout and rheumatism).

Or thus:

> Joints creak with *arthritic* pains.

Further:

> Goodwill addressed to *specific* ends aids the unfortunate.

Or thus:

> A loose tongue hurts its owner, for this *specific*
> Member is accustomed to injure the entire body.   5

Further:

> The lives of others are *paradigmatic* to me.

(As Cato says:

> The lives of others are our teachers.) (*Dist.,* III, 13)

Further:

> *Civic* acclaim pleases the hypocrite.

Further:

> No true man tolerates *sycophantic* attention.

27. I turn now to comparative adjectives. One can ornament verses with such varied words as *candidior, floridior, pauperior, uberior, humidior, lucidior, proximior, labilior, prosperior, languidior, callidior, fertilior, commodior, liberior, splendidior, utilior, debilior, mobilior, interior, flebilior, inferior, exterior, anterior, ulterior, asperior, simplicior, cognitor, horridior, sordidior,* and *nobilior.* [English equivalents used in this translation are *purer, flowerier, cheaper, faster, dewier, brighter, nearer, steeper, happier, feebler, craftier, healthier, gayer, freer, flashier, finer, weaker, closer, sadder, lower, outer, earlier, further, sharper,* *simpler, clearer, uglier, fouler,* and *nobler.*] The following are examples of the use of comparatives:

28. A *purer* blush struggles to the fore.

Further:

Spring decorates the earth with *flowerier* garb.

Further:

Light straw is found intertwined with *cheaper* thread.

Further:

The thief flees his pursuers with an ever *faster* pace.

Further:

The moon bedews the earth with a *dewier* fickleness.   5

Further:

The day glows with a *brighter* luster.

Further:

I took a place *nearer* to the king.

Further:

With an ever *steeper* decline the sun begins to seek out the west.

Further:

The *happier* laughter of the oracle saved the condemned man.

Further:

Good men prosper even when they exert *feebler* efforts.   10

Further:

The *craftier* nature of the fox puts him ahead of other animals.

Further:

The *healthier* seeds spring up readily from the soil.

Further:

A powerful man enjoys a *gayer* life.

Further:

Venus works with a *freer* will. (Matt., *Pyr. and Th.,* 46)

Further:

Generals thrive on *flashier* uniforms.   15

Further:

The wise man proves himself by his *finer* judgment.

Further:

The poor man noises about his woes with a *weaker* voice.

Further:

A faithless oracle counts on a *faster* escape.

Further:

A wise man always keeps his eyes on his *closer* friends.

Further:

With a *sadder* trumpet now, the enemy urges war.   20

Further:

Pluto holds oppressors in the *lower* lake.

Further:

Outer expression reveals anger.

Further:

His plan lacked any *earlier* success.

Further:

He puts off his promise with *further* delay.

Further:

The bramble bush is protected by its *sharper* thorns.   25

Further:

The harlot's view of life is *simpler.*

Further:

Dogma depends upon *clearer* teaching.

Further:

Old age is spoiled by its *uglier* wasting away.

Further:

A red-faced man delights in even *fouler* deceits.

Further:

The lion excels by virtue of his *nobler* rage.

(As Lucan says:

The rage of the lion is noble. [*Phars.,* VI, 487]

For it spares fallen enemies.)

29. Lest it seem, moreover, to any who are still hungering and thirsting after grammatical knowledge that the foregoing examples are false and improper uses of the comparatives on the ground that the comparative can be used only with an ablative of degree of difference (without a preposition) or with a noun preceded by *than* [*quam*], the adverb of comparison, I hasten to add that comparatives are construed in two ways: the complete comparative and the absolute comparative. **30.** The complete comparative construction is the comparative followed by an ablative indicating the other term of the comparison or by the adverb *than* [*quam*] and a noun. Nor is it idle to speak of "the other term of the comparison," for when any two words are compared in respect to some quality, that quality is attributed to both terms of the comparison, exceedingly to one, moderately to the other. **31.** When the comparative is used absolutely, the adjective is to be understood in its positive form with the intensifying adverb *quite* [*valde*]. We can see the usage in Statius's remark about Polynices:

That one quicker in pace and towering in stature. (*Theb.,* I, 414)

where "quicker" means "quite quick," or in Virgil:

Sadder and flooding those bright eyes with tears. (*Aen.,* I, 228)

where the sense is "quite sad." This usage of the comparative, it can be seen, is absolute in its construction, not in its meaning. It is absolute in its construction because it is not followed by some word completing the comparison; but it is not absolute in its meaning, for the intensifying adverb *quite* [*valde*] is understood.

32. Although other authorities speak of a threefold misuse of the comparative—in its meaning, its construction, and its function—what they mean must not be confused with what I am talking about. Thus in the pentameters above, I have not used the complete comparative but the absolute. So in the example "cheaper thread," "quite cheap thread" is the meaning. And a similar meaning is understood in the other verses.

33. There are, of course, many other adjectives which can be gracefully and elegantly joined to nouns in poetry, such as *succinctus, sophisticus, propheticus, prodigus,* and *vicarius* [English equivalents used in this translation are *terse, glib, prophetic, lavish,* and *substituting.*] Here are some examples:

> In words and verses "a *terse* brevity suffices.
> If a poem lacks brevity, it lacks poetry." (I, 54, 23–24)

Again, concerning a cowled hypocrite,

> His *glib* piety and his heart disagree, for
> His smug appearance wars with his inner wolfishness.

Further:

> Deceit is evident in one's appearance;   5
> The face, *prophetic* of evil, lays bare criminal intent.

Further:

> Red and white mingle in my beloved's face;
> Her rosy little lips are *lavish* in promises of delight.

Further:

> Let the Muse forgo the sword, let Pallas,
> *Substituting* for the sword, make strong by strength of words
> That which is less when done by force of arms.   10

34. Here is an example using the word *protruding,* which fits an Epicure well. For such a one has a protruding belly that makes him look like a pregnant woman. The mouth of this fellow "who was born to eat the fruits of the earth" (Hor., *Ep.,* I, 2, 27) is always wide open. His god is his gut, his glory is in confusion, and his end is ruin. His gluttonous appetite for pleasure grows so every day that his belly is swollen like the testicles of Saturn with an about-to-be-born Venus. The Epicure has such an innate taste for concoctions that he heaps delicacy upon delicacy until his food runs riot with every sauce known to man. If his huge paunch were the precursor of a body whose other parts were scaled proportionately, his monstrous bulk would stretch into infinity. Thus one could say of such a man:

> He thrives on gluttony and the *protruding* mass of
> His stomach heralds the approach of its rumbling owner.

35. If, moreover, I have introduced a number of examples akin to the subject under discussion, it has been done as a diversion to refresh dainty ears and must certainly not be imputed to artless digression, lest I would seem to be guilty of that fault which Horace denounces:

> One or two purple patches which shine far and wide
> Are often sewed onto works that begin gravely and
> Promise great things. (*Poet.,* 14)

And we have it on Tully's authority (*De inventione,* I, 46) that a little monotony goes a long way, while variety relieves boredom. "Thus we give arms to both sides" (Ovid, *Rem.,* 50) as pleasant defenses against boredom and mix weighty passages with light-hearted ones or the serious with the jocular so long as such mingling never contradicts the original purpose of the work. As Horace says in one place:

> It is not enough that a poem be beautiful;
> It must also be charming. (*Poet.,* 99)

Or in another place;

> He who mixed the profitable with the pleasant, delighting
> As well as instructing his reader, won every vote. (*Poet.,* 344)

36. There is, furthermore, an infinite number of substantives and adjectives that contribute manifold charms to a work and whose elegant joining together could be pointed out. But an infinity is the stepmother of learning and the girlfriend of confusion (for an infinity cannot be catalogued by any method of calculation), so for these reasons I will pass on to examples of how verbs are to be used. First I will discuss verbs of the first conjugation, which are also infinite. But to further teaching and learning, I will use a skillfully selected finite group of this infinite variety of verbs. No one, moreover, would expect these examples to be drawn from any verbs except those which have been the least corrupted by being tossed to and fro in the speech of the vulgar. **37.** And again, because in many of the passages above the use of examples has been extensive, for the present a few brief examples must suffice. I will consider these verbs: *pilleo, prospero, paupero, perpetuo, purpuro, festivo, intitulo, syncopo, confisco, integro, zelotypo, apocopo, inebrio, inesco, exorbito, mendico, phalero, intumulo, intimo, amico, adoro, insimulo, altero, adopto, illaqueo, intrico, importo, sordido, mancipo, morbito, emancipo, dilapido,* etc. [The English equivalents used in this translation are *cap, make prosperous, impoverish, perpetuate, adorn, embellish, praise, sound, confiscate, repair, cuckold, cut short, intoxicate, enchant, go astray, go abegging, dress up, reveal, point to, love, worship, defame, alter, adopt, ensnare, entangle, convey, pollute, fulfill, sicken, cast off, destroy,* etc.] There are, of course, many others, but the shortness of the list will be offset by the ample use of examples:

> A golden covering *caps* distinguished heads.

Or this:

> A mystic headdress *caps* a venerable head.
> The fickleness of fortune may *make* adverse changes *prosperous.*

Further:

> Lavish tables can *impoverish* noble houses.

Further:

> Good fortune is not able to *perpetuate* faith in herself.   5

Further:

> A pleasant tint of roses *adorns* her ivory face.

Or this:

> An ever bright redness *adorns* her precious little lips.

Further:

> Golden tableware *embellishes* the simplest meal.

Further:

> Even a renowned author may *praise* a bad book.

Further:

> A thick penis *sounds* sweetly in intercourse.   10

Further:

> A king customarily *confiscates* the property of his subjects.

Further:

> Public acclaim *repairs* damaged reputations.

Further:

> For a small gift you can *cuckold* Rufinus.

38. Here is an example of the use of the verb *cut short*. It concerns two rivals for the same woman's favors, one of whom is discovered by the other in the act of intercourse:

> One rival fearing the other *cuts short* his thrust
> And his delving tool loses the reward it has gained.

Further, concerning Rufinus at whose eyes a bleary rheum gnaws:

> Making love to a prostitute *intoxicates* him;
> Indeed, the charms of a common old whore *enchant* his bleary
>   eyes.

Further:

> When love gains sway, virtue *goes astray,*   5
> Reason sick with passion *goes abegging,*
> And lawless pursuits replace lawful ones.

Further:

Hypocrites *dress up* evil intent with a pious mien.

(As Juvenal says,

Mouthing chaste sentiments,
They wiggle their rear ends.) (*Sat.,* II, 21)

Further:

Moderate use of costly ornaments *reveals* the riches of the face.

Further:

Anger bent on injuring others *points to* a deadly evil.

Further:

The wise man *loves* that task which advances him. 10

As Statius says:

First Oenides *worships* his deity with his usual prayer. (*Theb.,*
III, 470)

Further:

The rake *defames* the honest man with false charges.

(As Ovid states:

I hope I may be called hasty in *defaming* my husband with false
charges!) (*Her.,* VI, 21)

Further:

Fate, keeping faith with no one, always *alters* man's lot.

Further:

The lover *adopts* the terms laid down by the beloved. 15

Further:

Venus the conqueror can *ensnare* the free heart.

Further:

Artful makeup enhances beauty, but the poor coquette,
Striving to be pleasing becomes *entangled* in a mass of hair.

Further:

A sorrowful expression *conveys* the idea of misfortune.

Further:

> Talk suitable to a redhead *pollutes* decent company.   20

Further:

> A trust that is not misplaced *fulfills* promises as sacred vows.

Further:

> A pestilence in the air *sickens* the heedless.

Further:

> A disrespectful son *casts off* authority and, renouncing
> His father, glories in squandering his father's wealth.

Further:

> The harmless ox *is destroyed* as a religious sacrifice.   25

Further:

> Caesar's wars *come before* he is of battle age.

(For as Ovid says:

> Caesars show a valor in advance of their years.) (*Ars,* I, 184)

Further:

> Rhetorical figures *beautify* a poem.

Further:

> Vendôme's tribe *soldiers* at the punch bowl.

Further:

> A dishonest mind *usurps* the role of the learned.   30

Further:

> Do not *start* something that you cannot finish.

Or thus:

> Shamelessness *starts* with a passionate lover

(that is, he takes away the beginnings of shame). Further:

> An instructive tongue *instills* teachings in a pupil's ears.

Further:

> A noble father *ennobles* an ignoble son.

Further:

> A ruddy heart *beats* within a ruddy breast. 35

Further:

> Waylaying a man, love *frees* him from the tyranny of decorum.

Further:

> Loath *to be disinherited,* he outfathers his father. (Matt., *Tob.,* 236)

Further:

> Rufinus is afraid *to bandy* verses with me.

Further:

> Rufinus *boasts* that Thaïs is his.

Further:

> Venus *contends* with her adversary reason. 40

Further:

> Thaïs *shits,* and playing the repressor stains her ass,
> Her buttocks thus pressed groan at her action.

Further:

> Even if the bloom on a maid's cheek *lasts* another day,
> Time always *withers* the flower and *fades* the rose.

Further:

> A gossipy tongue repeats, *broadcasts,* blabs things
> Best left unsaid, for it is zealous to publish hidden things. 45

(As Horace says:

> Let no one make known private conversations. [*Ep.,* I, 5, 26]

Or Boethius in his tract *On the Categorical Syllogism:* "An advanced philosophical treatise often makes known things suitable for young ears.")[34] Further:

> A dazzling love affair *weakens* the will to study. 50
> The spirit of envy *hexes* every good thing.

(Or as in the *Bucolics:*

> Some evil eye *hexes* my young lambs. (Virg., *Ecl.,* III, 104)

For envy is hatred of another's happiness.) Further:

> A knave is eager *to appropriate* others' goods for himself.

Further:

An expressive face often *reveals* knavish deeds. '   55

(As Ovid says:

How hard it is for a guilty man
Not to be given away by his looks!) (*Met.,* II, 447)

Further:

An evil tongue can *shred* an outstanding reputation.

Further, an example of the verb *flourish* is given earlier in my description of Davus:

He makes the particular vices of his own evil heart
Flourish in a thousand innocent breasts. (I, 53, 85)

Further:

The girl *scoffs at* the foul endeavors of a pimp.

39. There are, in addition, numerous verbs of this and other conjugations. Since most of these are in common use and since it is easy to explain their usage in a way akin to the foregoing examples, the listener should construct illustrations of these verbs similar to the preceding examples, making whatever changes in the ending as are demanded by the verb's conjugation. For after all, it is not good that one should always depend upon the examples of others. If the listeners follow my advice, they will never be trapped in a usage that depends upon another's scanty knowledge.

40. Further, in the preceding examples the verse has been developed as pentameters rather than hexameters, so that it might be described by the epithet elegiac, a term which applies to both elegies and pentameters. Also in the preceding vision, patterns and examples of the elegiac can be seen and thus instilled in my listeners. And again, just as it is easier to inflict a wound than to heal one, so it is easier to write the first line of an elegiac distich than the second, since the pentameter must complete the thought of the hexameter. Thus it is fitting that I treat more informally that part of the distich which is easier for my listeners, so that versifiers can fit their pentameters to their preceding hexameters by a sort of in-grafting.

41. I have, moreover, illustrated right usage in lines of poetry rather than just in phrases, so that I might show the listener the full effect of a line of poetry and not just a mere phrase.

42. There are, furthermore, certain comic braggarts[35] and purveyors of feminine apparel that, acting under the impulse of a silly audacity, presume to caw like crows and twist the meaning of words like this: "It is redolent of harm; he was prudent in prodigality; he is glorified by evil." Now as a safeguard against this sort of lax usage, the versifier must be well versed in the connotations of words, lest he dare effect a forced wedding by joining together words whose connotations are so mutually repugnant that they almost cry out for separation rather than union. For in these expressions contradictory notions are yoked together. When anyone says "redolent of harm," these very words contain a mutual disagreement in their connotations, and no reasonable idea can be inferred from such an expression. In this case "harm" has a pejorative connotation, and "redolent" a favorable one. This sort of judgment must be made for similar expressions; for example, when one says, "a redheaded faithfulness," we have two contradictory notions joined together. In this expression the connotation of one word denies that of the other, for the word "redheaded" excludes the notion of faithfulness; which we have the common proverb, "If you ever see a man who is redheaded and faithful, sing praises to the Lord." There is also a contradiction in terms when words that are not in themselves contradictory are joined together so as to produce a contradiction.

43. Further, the teachings of this treatise exclude "those verses devoid of any matter and mere trifling songs" (Hor., *Poet.*, 322). These silly collections of trifles that please the ears only through their melody are like jesters and mimes. They are like a corpse without life, like a wine cellar without wine, a bundle of wheat without grain, food with no spices. They are like inflated bladders whose imprisoned air escaping in a windy hiss produces a sound whose sole beauty comes from the windy swelling of the bladders. In this same category is "leonine verse" whose charm is as unknown as the reason for its name.[36] But certain flute players and others unskilled in the practice of the ways of a lion boast greatly about these verses. **44.** But if melody is excluded from such trifling songs, then these verses would be like vagrants and freed slaves; they would be like the pruned trunk of a fig tree, a piece of useless wood. **45.** Not all verses of this sort, however, ought to be dismissed so lightly; rather only those without a hint of any real meaning should be stigmatized as vagrants. Such verses are called dry and bloodless. As Horace says:

> Overcautious and fearful of the storm, he creeps along the coast.
> (*Poet.*, 28)

Consequently, one most often ought to practice writing elegiac verses, and only very occasionally trifling songs. For there is little or no refinement in songs; it is as Juvenal says:

> In this world a black swan is a rare bird. (*Sat.*, VI, 165)

Finally, anyone who can write elegies well can also write songs well, but not the other way around.

46. Certain ragged words, moreover, should never appear in a metrical composition. It is as if they have been anathematized and are no longer fit company for others. Among these banned words are such words as *poro* (further), *autem* (however), *quoque* (also), and expressions of this same syntactic category or meaning. These words, since they detract from the grace of the entire poem, ought to be eliminated from poetry. There are, to be sure, a few adverbs and conjunctions which ought to be employed in poetry, but these should be used only when absolutely necessary.

III

QUALITY OF THE EXPRESSION

1. There remains to be discussed the third section of the division made above in the Prologue, namely the quality or the manner of the expression. A verse quite often derives its gracefulness more from its manner of expression than from the substance of what is said, as this example makes clear:

My lord, my husband, my brother were you. (Ovid, *Her.*, III, 52)

Neither beauty of sentiment nor exterior verbal grace makes this little verse elegant, but rather its mode of expression. Hence three qualities distinguish poetry: polished language (*verba polita*), figurative expression (*dicendi color*), and the inner sentiment (*interior favus*). There are three figures of expression in this verse; first there is *zeugma* at the end because the verb "were," which occurs only in the final clause, is understood for all three clauses. Then there is the rhetorical color repetition, for the pronoun "my" is used three times. Finally, one could point out *dialiton* or *asyndeton,* for this sentence has several independent clauses one after the other and no coordinating conjunction. **2.** To take an example from the realm of physical objects, even though the material of, say, a statue may be rough and of no particular value, it may please greatly when it has been shaped through the efforts of an artist. It is similar in poetry; the material—the language—is rough and awkward until it is arranged through the artful employment of some scheme, trope, or rhetorical color. Now, since the third section of the division made earlier concerns schemes, tropes, and rhetorical colors, these matters which pertain to the skill and discipline of versification ought to be explained. This discussion will treat schemes first. **3.** "Schemes," as Isidore states in his *Etymologies,* mean "figures" (*Etym.*, I, 36, 1). Although one can more often find seventeen figures listed,[37] only those which can be used most elegantly in the practice of versification ought to be discussed: namely, *zeugma, hypozeuxis, anaphora, epanalepsis, anadiplosis, epizeuxis, paronomasia, paranomeon, schesis onomaton, homoeoteleuton, polyptoton, polysyndeton,* and *dialiton* or *asyndeton.* **4.** Since the figures *zeugma* and *hypozeuxis* were discussed at the beginning of this work, what follows concerns *anaphora.*

5. *Anaphora* is the repetition of the first words of two verses which come one right after the other, as in Juvenal's statement about Pontia:

Two at once, you foul viper, you most savage of women?
Two at once? (*Sat.,* VI, 641)

What follows is a homemade example about Rufus and his girl friend Rufa:

Ah Rufus, Rufa values money more than she does you.
Ah Rufus, the town whore empties your purse.

6. *Epanalepsis* is the repetition of the first word of a line as the last word also. We see this in Juvenal:

Growth of avarice keeps pace with wealth's growth. (*Sat.,* XIV, 139)

7. *Anadiplosis* is repetition which uses a word occurring as the last word in one line as the first word in the next line, as in Virgil's *Bucolics:*

Let Tityrus be an Orpheus,
An Orpheus in the woods, an Arion among dolphins. (*Ecl.,* VIII, 55)

All three of these figures may be seen in this homemade example:

Unable is love to count the costs, to economize unable;
Unable is love to separate the worthy from the unworthy.

See, there is *anaphora* in this example, for the word "unable" is used at the beginning of both lines; there is also *epanalepsis,* for the word "unable" is used at the beginning of one line and also repeated as the last word in that same line. There is, moreover, *anadiplosis,* for the same word is used at the end of one line and repeated at the beginning of the next.

8. *Epizeuxis* is the immediate repetition of the same word to achieve more effective expression, as in Virgil:

Thus, thus it is pleasing to seek darkness. (*Aen.,* IV, 660)

Or thus concerning the feigned flight of a sweetheart so that her lover will be greatly upset:

Flora flees, flees so that she may be brought back;
The face hides the heart; fleeing in body, she remains in heart.

9. *Paronomasia* is the similar sound at the beginning or at the end of words appearing in the same line. Thus there can be two forms of this figure. Often we have the agreement of initial letters or syllables in this manner:

> Fame fosters status seeking in lunatics not lovers;
> To deprecate decency is the mark of moral fault.

Or we can see it in my verse about high-living monks whose dark misdeeds are buried in the cloak of their false religion and who belch colorful thanks to the Most High from the many feasts imprisoned in the jailhouse of their bellies; about them someone has written:

> They live not to breathe forth Gloria in Excelsis, but
> Garlic in excess; they speak of salmon more than of Solomon.[38]

Again there may be *paronomasia* because of the agreement of final syllables as in the following example which is a comparison of a king to a high priest or of a highwayman to a monk. Thus approval is given to the high priest or the monk, while fault is imputed to the king or to the highwayman:

> This one heals, that one steals; this one teaches,
> That one leeches. This one is pious, that one is
> Impious; this one is mild, that one is wild.

10. Next comes *paranomeon*. *Paranomeon* is the repetition of the initial letter or syllable of immediately adjacent words. There are three varieties of this figure. Sometimes it occurs at the beginning of a line, sometimes in the middle, and sometimes at the end. Virgil's *Aeneid* affords an example at the beginning of a line:

> Impious rage within
> Savagely sitting squarely on his arms. (*Aen.*, I, 294)

Here three adjacent words "sitting," "squarely," and "savagely" at the beginning of the line have the same semivowel *s* as their initial sound. The same figure may occur in the middle of a line, as in Virgil:

> Some on limpid lakes living, some in thorny lands.[39] (*Aen.*, IV, 526)

In this example three words "living," "limpid," and "lakes" coming in the middle of the line all begin with the letter *l*; thus this is the figure under discussion. The expression is said to be in the middle of the line because it comes between each end of the line. Finally there is *paranomeon* at the end of a line, as in Virgil:

> A fate made known to me solely
> By clairvoyant Cassandra's canticle. (*Aen.*, III, 183)

The following homemade example concerns two rivals tiring of their common mistress:

> Love lingering long torments dolts desiring debauchery;
> But still a lover rarely receives rivals with good grace.

As Ovid says:

> Neither a mistress nor a throne
> Lasts long when shared with another. (*Ars,* III, 564)

Here is another example about a beggar woman seeking money from a king for her sick husband:

> Gracious governor, grant some sweet succor;
> My mate molders. Helping him honors you.
> Be blessedly bountiful. Give gold generously.

11. *Schesis onomaton* is a series of nouns, each joined to a different adjective, as in Statius:

> Horseman Iphis, foot soldier Argus, chariot driver Abas lay dying.
> (*Theb.,* VIII, 448)

Or this about the fickleness of Fortune:

> A passion for casting lots is a detestable habit,
> A treacherous system, a lamentable joke,
> An untrustworthy refuge, a false faith.

12. *Homoeoteleuton* is a group of words ending in the same sound, as in Horace:

> Hail! sail! prevail! But break not your trust. (*Ep.,* I, 13, 19)

Or thus:

> Let Rufus grumble, rumble, and mumble at
> Me, I myself know that my verse is mine.[40]

The first line exemplifies this figure because the verbs have similar endings; the second line can be called *polyptoton.*

13. *Polyptoton* occurs when a number of cases are marked by different inflectional endings, as in the example above.

14. *Polysyndeton* is joining parallel phrases with a number of coordinating conjunctions, as in Virgil:

> Acamus and Thoas and Achilles and Neoptolamus, etc. (*Aen.,* II, 263)

Or thus:

> And by physical assault and by fraud you harm others, Redhead;
> Indeed, red hair is the outward and visible sign of a fraud.

15. *Dialiton* (or *asyndeton*) is a figure just the opposite of the preceding, for here no coordinating conjunction joins a number of parallel phrases, as in Virgil:

> Quick, bring torches, set sail, man the oars. (*Aen.*, IV, 594)

Or thus:

> The disease of love is most pleasing,
> Its poison is most sweet, its pain is pleasing,
> Its suffering is delightful, its malady is agreeable.

Or thus:

> Love is an unjust judge, Love is not able to discern rank,
> Love binds all with the same bonds.

Dialiton ought to be distinguished from *schesis onomaton,* although each figure has a number of parallel phrases. They differ in this way: *schesis onomaton* is a series of nouns with a verb never or rarely interposed, nor are conjunctions within the series necessarily excluded; *dialiton,* on the other hand, admits verbs but not a conjunction between parallel phrases.

16. Furthermore, it should be noted that I am not going to fail to mention what Isidore asserted about the figure *paranomeon* when he said, "If there are more than three alliterating words, then it will not be this figure but a quite different one."[41] Then he himself cites as an example of this very figure Ennius's line:

> O Tite, tute, Tati, tibi, tanta, tyranne, tulisti!
> (Titus Tatius, tyrant, thou took terrible troubles to thyself.) (*Ann.*,
>   113)

17. Let my gentle listeners expect nothing more from these foregoing examples than that they may respond to them by matching their examples to mine so that they may equal the examples which have been given. Now, just a little earlier in this work I sought a truce with my critics, so no verses should be taken as asserting anything about persons whom I know. They are intended only to give examples so that the listeners in turn may make models and examples to match those I have given.

18. Next comes a discussion of tropes. Trope is a Greek word which may be translated as "figurative speech" (*modus locutionis*). Tropes, however, may add to grace of expression without adding to beauty of sentiment. Although there are thirteen tropes,[42] we must consider the ones which should especially be recommended to the verse writer. The first to be discussed is *metaphor.*

19. *Metaphor* is the assumed transfer of the characteristic of one word to another. This trope is divided into four parts: from animate to animate, from inanimate to inanimate, from animate to inanimate, and from inanimate to animate. **20.** Here is an example of from animate to animate from Virgil:

> He mounted the winged steed.[43]

The epithet suitable to birds, which do have wings, is attributed to a horse; both, of course, are animate. Or thus:

> Rufus, impoverished of ideas, caws. In such wise does he
> Distribute the treasures of his tongue and of his deceitful mind.

This example is similar to the other because what is proper for a crow, that is, to caw, is attributed to Rufus.

21. The second type of *metaphor* is from inanimate to inanimate, in which the quality of one inanimate thing is attributed to another by a transfer of signification. Here is an example from Virgil:

> The hive buzzes with activity
> And the fragrant honey is sweet with thyme. (*Georg.,* IV, 169)

In this example an epithet of flowers, that is, "fragrant," is attributed to honey; both of these, of course, are inanimate. Similarly, one could have an example such as this concerning some maid's pride over the flowering of beauty:

> In her expression beauty of face
> Contends with the blemish of pride.

Or thus:

> Spring shines from a face passing rich in charm,
> And the winter of the mind turns green,
> Yet the countenance savors of a defect.

The above figure may be seen in this example, for that which is proper to flowers, that is, to turn green, is attributed to winter; both of these are inanimate.

22. The third type of *metaphor* is from inanimate to animate; Statius's description of Adrastus provides an example:

> Stripped of the better sex, he flowered through his daughters.
> (*Theb.,* I, 393)

Or again this from Ovid concerning Galatea:

> More blooming than the snowy meadow, etc. (*Met.,* XIII, 790)[44]

In these examples that which is proper to inanimate things, that is "to flower" and "to bloom," is by transfer applied to the animate beings Adrastus and Galatea. Or thus:

A comely maiden, her virtue intact, blossoms delightfully;
The bloom on her cheeks exceeds riches commonly given.

This is a *metaphor* because that which is proper to an inanimate thing, that is, "to blossom," is applied to a maiden.

23. The fourth kind of *metaphor* is from animate to inanimate, as in Statius's line:

Even the grass of the field lies stricken by his hisses. (*Theb.*, V, 528)

And again Ovid's line:

The sea billows do not know which master to obey. (*Tr.*, I, 2, 26)

There is *metaphor* here since "to lie stricken" and "to know," which apply to animate objects, are attributed to the grass of the field and to the sea billows. Or thus concerning a shipwreck:

The thunder crashes, the sea roars its fury, the waves
Grow haughty, and night is born in the midst of fateful day.

24. Thus four types of *metaphor* may be distinguished. Some *metaphors,* moreover, have reciprocal or reversible terms; some do not. Virgil's "oars of wings" is a reversible *metaphor,* for it is possible, reversing its terms, to say "wings of oars." Certain *metaphors* may not be reversed; in the example above, "Even the grass of the field lies stricken by his hisses," no reversal is possible. This trope because of its special qualities has a singular preeminence among other tropes; the versifier ought to use it often, for it gives metrical verse an especial grace.

25. Next comes a discussion of *antithesis.*[45] *Antithesis* is a contrast in which opposites are pitted against each other, as in Ovid:

Cold things strove with hot, and moist with dry, soft
Things with hard, things having weight with weightless things.
(*Met.*, I, 19)

Or this example of a prodigal confuting a miser:

I lunch, you fast; I give, you ask; I rejoice, you lament;
I drink, you thirst; I spend, you save; I hope, you fear.

There are four varieties of this trope: *antithesis* in phrases, in adjectives, in substantives, and in verbs. **26.** Ovid affords an example of *antithesis* in phrases:

She betrayed her father; I snatched Thoas from death.
She deserted her native land; my Lemnos holds me still. (*Her.*, VI, 135)

27. Here is an example of *antithesis* in adjectives, also from Ovid:

> Cold things strove with hot, etc. (*Met.,* I, 19)

28. Here is an example of *antithesis* in substantives from Bernard's *Cosmography:*

> In the stars are seen the poverty of Codrus, the wealth of Croesus,
> Also the shamelessness of Paris and the modesty of Hippolytus.
>   (*Cosm.,* I, 41)

29. *Antithesis* in verbs is seen in these from an example above, "I lunch, you fast," and so forth. Or in this example of a soldier confuting a cleric:

> I dare, you dread; I put to flight, you give ground;
> I fight, you yield; I rise up, you lie down;
> I prevail, you fail; I pursue, you hide.

Note that no part of the above verses lacks *antithesis,* for each set of words is combined to produce an *antithesis.*

30. Next is *metonymy,* a transposition which may be of three types: the invention may be used for the inventor or vice versa; the possession for the possessor or vice versa, and the thing contained for the container or vice versa. But since the first two types are employed less frequently by authors, this discussion will treat only the third type, that is, the container for the thing contained or vice versa. **31.** This trope, moreover, is reciprocal or reversible. The container for the contained is used as Statius has Tydeus say:

> Behold this field smoking far and wide from my sword, (*Theb.,* II,
>   702)

for he refers to the corpses in the field. And, similarly, concerning the gods above who are deprived of the benefit of hospitality on earth:

> The gods above are deprived of the honor of hospitality,
> The heavens themselves could blush at earth's denial.

32. The contained is used for the container, as in Statius:

> But when rage and bravery heedless of life unleash passion.
>   (*Theb.,* VIII, 406)

"Bravery" is used for "the brave man" in which it is contained. Lucan has a similar example:

> No faith ever chose unfortunate friends. (*Phars.,* VIII, 535)

The meaning is "no faithful man." A similar example occurs in the topological description above:

> The oak, nourisher of swine, bows to the sky
> And pays respect vowed to her special diety, Jupiter.[46]

that is, "the sky which contains Jupiter to whom the oak is consecrated."

33. Next is *synecdoche,* the use of a part for the whole or vice versa, as in Horace when he is speaking to his book, which he has personified:

> If someone should chance to ask my age,
> Tell him I have completed forty-five Decembers. (*Ep.,* I, 20, 26)

that is, years. Similarly:

> A woman, born to criminality, yearns to injure;
> She is a creature potent in guile, the seed of evil.

34. The part is used for the whole, for what is said in a specific sense is meant to be understood in a general sense. For as Ovid says:

> Do not charge all women with the faults of a few. (*Ars,* III, 9)

35. There is a second type of *synecdoche,* as in this line from Virgil's *Bucolics:*

> This is the most beautiful year. (*Ecl.,* III, 57)

Here he means "part of the year," that is, "spring." The following example concerns Rufus's loose sex life:

> Rufus's child is a scarlet reproach, for just as the vessel
> Betrays the potter, the father sins in the child's face.

Here, because of the face the whole person is called a "scarlet reproach."

36. The nature of *circumlocution* (*periphrasis*) is discussed in the section below where rearranging the material is treated.

37. A definition of *epithet* was given above. There are, however, three forms of *epithet:* through phrases, verbs, and adjectives. **38.** An example of *epithet* through a phrase is seen in Statius:

> The alder, friend of the sea,
> And the elm not inhospitable to vines. (*Theb.,* VI, 106)

39. *Epithet* through verbs is seen in my own homemade example of a topological description:

> Here blossoms bloom
> Sweetly, herbs grow vigorously, trees leaf profusely.
> Fruits abound, birds chatter, streams murmur, and
> The gentle air warms all. (I, 111, 48)

40. *Epithet* through phrases also is seen in the same topological description:

> Pleasant is the stream's
> Sound, harmonious the birdsongs, etc. (I, 111, 53)

41. Bernard's *Cosmography* affords an example of *epithet* through adjectives:

> The ruddy turtledove, the savory salmon, the roe-rich shad,
> The short smelt, the long barbel, the wide plaice. (*Cosm.,* I, 437)

42. *Metalepsis* or *climax* is climactic arrangement of clauses so that the last word of the first clause is the first word of the subsequent clause; an example is seen in Virgil's *Bucolics:*

> After the wolf runs the fierce lioness,
> The wolf himself after the goat,
> After the flowering clover runs the wanton goat. (*Ecl.,* II, 63)

In this example the last word of the first clause is the initial word of the next clause according to grammatical construction, but not according to metrical pattern. But what is lacking in the metrical pattern may be supplied through the grammatical construction. (One may have *metalepsis* in both the metrical pattern and the grammatical construction.) Here is a very clear example of this:

> Anger leads to strife, strife to battle, battle to death,
> Death to tears, tears to prayers, prayers to comfort.

43. Next is *allegory,* a special mode of discourse in which the sense differs from the meaning of the words, as in this example from Virgil's *Bucolics:*

> I have sent ten golden apples, I will send another ten tomorrow.
> (*Ecl.,* III, 70)

For here, according to Isidore (*Etym.,* I, 47, 22), by the golden apples are meant the ten eclogues of his poem, the *Bucolics.* Or this example about a handsome and haughty man:

> The nutshell is at odds with the nutmeat, so is a wintry heart
> Ignorant of what a sunny face proclaims.

Here, by "the nutshell" is to be understood the "sunny expression"; by "the nutmeat" is to be understood "a wintry heart," that is, haughtiness. Now I give an example of my own in verse concerning Milo and Afra:

> The vine lacks fruit; never lifting hairy branches skyward,
> It creeps along the ground with paltry little tendrils. (Matt., *Milo,*
> 177)

The vine's lacking fruit is to be understood as Milo's scorn for the barren Afra. Although there are seven types of this trope,[47] what follows must concern not their explication, but rather *enigma*.

44. *Enigma* is an obscure meaning concealed in a wrapper of words, as in Virgil:

> Tell me in what land the sky is not more than
> Three ells broad, and you will be my great Apollo. (*Ecl.*, III, 105)

Or thus:

> I shall soon give birth to the mother who bore me,[48]

which may be understood as referring to ice. Similarly, here is an example referring to Narcissus:

> Loving what he has, he seeks what he loves.
> His love is such that gaining his end, he loses it.

This seems impossible except when it is understood as speaking of Narcissus's love for himself.

45. Now that figures and tropes have been described—and the description seemed quite indispensable for this little treatise—a discussion of rhetorical colors might properly follow except for the fact that they have already been explained by someone else.[49] So lest this treatise seem to be a patchwork quilt of others' rags when my own resources are certainly sufficient for me, I will omit any discussion of rhetorical colors. Besides, a discussion of figures and tropes does not exclude rhetorical colors. For certain figures and tropes correspond to certain rhetorical colors, and a list matching these ought to be given. There are, then, these pairs which seem to go together naturally: *antithesis* and *contentio, anaphora* and *duplicatio, paronomasia* and *annominatio, epanalepsis* and *repetitio, schesis onomaton* and *membrum orationis* or *articulus, dialiton* and *dissolutum, polysyndeton* and *conjunctum*, and *metalepsis* or *climax* and *gradatio*. Here is another example of this last trope:

> Fame means praise, praise reward, reward reflection,
> Reflection inspiration, inspiration poetry, poetry work.

46. Let no one think that this sort of verse "repeated ten times might be a source of pleasure" (Hor., *Poet.*, 365). For whoever pursues verses of this sort, which employ only the single device of the last word of one clause being repeated in some form as the first word in the next clause, may well work day and night to achieve a string of ten such clauses yet would seem to me to merit the title versifier more on account of the difficulty of the work than on account of the elegance of it. Thus since "it does not befall every man to go to Corinth" (Hor., *Ep.*, I, 17, 36),[50] that lisper Rufus, who is accustomed to being a Tyresias in elegiacs and a

Polyphemus in frivolous song, does not dare put his abilities to the test. Good taste is the only judge of elegance, and correctness and difficulty are judged by performance.

47. At present a list of the names assigned the rhetorical colors will be sufficient to show the listener what remains to inquire into. Their names are as follows: *repetitio, conversio, complexio, traductio, contentio, exclamatio, ratiocinatio, sententia, contrarium, membrum orationis* or *articulus, similiter cadens, similiter desinens, commixtio, annominatio, subjectio, gradatio, diffinitio, transitio, correptio, occupatio, disjunctio, conjunctum, adjunctum, conduplicatio, commutatio, dubitatio, dissolutio, praecisio,* and *conclusio.*[51]

48. In the dream-vision mentioned earlier it appeared to me that Elegy, as an aid to memory, hammered into my understanding the three parts of the division mentioned above. But although:

> It is no less virtue to seek than to find invention,
> It is pleasing to have sung those things I have sung.

For:

> Wisdom that pleases is wealth; it is multiplied
> And it increases what is given; silent, it cannot multiply.

49. It should be noted that the aforementioned division was not made by means of sets of opposites. For the existence of virtue does not exclude that of strength, nor the existence of a rose that of a lily, nor a hyacinth a daisy, and "those things which have little power taken singly, please greatly when joined together" (Ovid., *Rem.,* 420). So it is in poetry; one figure does not exclude another or one color another. On the contrary, a group of colors pleases better. For the aggregate is beautiful, as each part adds its particular charm to the whole, and that whole appeals to us with beauty allied to beauty. Thus it is possible to have the three parts of the division noted earlier in the same verse, as in Statius's line:

> A short-lived kingship spares not the populace. (*Theb.,* II, 446)

We have here the beauty of the line's inner meaning according to the first part of the division, for it is a universal sentiment. In accord with the second part the words are elegant, and in accord with the third part there is beauty in the manner of the speech. For there is a type of *metaphor,* since that which a quality of animate beings, that is, "to spare," is attributed metaphorically to an inanimate thing, that is, "kingship." Or it is possible that here there is *metonymy,* for the possession is used in place of the possessor, that is, "kingship" for "king." **50.** Furthermore, if a comparison might be drawn between words and things or words and living beings, we may take as an example a person whom we might consider according to three different criteria: mind, physical beauty, and propriety of mode of life. Here, to be sure, one does not exclude the others; they are compared better taken one with the other. Also, taken this way, they have a greater power of pleasing. So it is in poetry; the beauty of inner sentiments, the exterior elegance of the words, and the quality of the expression gracefully reinforce each other. One of these characteristics without having the others allied with it is rarely used alone in poetry, and then only with difficulty.

51. Further, lest the course of this introduction might seem to some to wander into the fault of superfluity—for "virtue is a mean between two vices, equally remote from both extremes," as Horace says (*Ep.*, I, 18, 9), and "in the middle way is the safest path" (Ovid, *Met.*, II, 137)—what follows is put forward as a sufficient explanation of the three members of the aforementioned division. The understanding of meaning discussed above in relation to the attributes of a person or an action applies to the first member. In the example of adjectives listed according to their different endings, the second member, elegance of words, is clearly explained; the third member, the quality of the expression, is described in the discussion of figures and tropes. **52.** But if by chance some yokel presumes to cackle, saying that in the division made above the same thing is listed over and over because the first part, the second part, and the third part each concern elegance in metrical verse, here is his answer: the first, the second, and the third part do each concern elegance in poetry, but as parts of a threefold system. For although there is similarity in what is treated, there is diversity in how it is treated. In the first part the elegance of the inner meaning is treated, in the second the elegance of the words, and in the third the quality of the expression. Hence not just any order can properly be assigned to these three members. For just as in the division referred to earlier, sentiments come first, words follow, and the quality of the expression is given as the third member; so in the exercise of the poetic faculty the conceptual realization of meaning comes first, then language, the interpreter of understanding, follows, then the orderly arrangement of the treatment. Thus the conception of the meaning comes first, next comes the working out of the language, then the ordering of the treatment or the disposition of the material.[52]

IV

EXECUTION OF THE MATERIAL

1. What follows concerns the working out of the material, an area in which the poorly instructed often act like fools and wander shamefully away from the narrow path of true learning. In school exercises they grind out stories, ransacking poems word for word for images, just as if they were setting out to write a verse commentary upon their authors. But those who sin in ignorance ought to be forgiven, for perhaps they are corrupted by corrupt teachers. So let them be consoled with this: following the material they do, they seek to emulate the customary handling of events, and thus they write with propriety or with the semblance of propriety. For "not even a drudging translator proposes to render a passage word for word" (Hor., *Poet.,* 133). **2.** For there are certain words which, almost as if they were condemned words, ought not to appear in some contexts. Through the influence of these words an entire passage is blemished, and not a scintilla of beauty is added by their presence. This we have on the authority of Homer, of whom Horace says:

> He abandons those things which he despairs
> Of being able to beautify by his handling. (*Poet.,* 150)

Things about which too little has been said in the sources ought to be filled out, awkward passages ought to be revised into something better, and superfluous ones omitted entirely.

3. Furthermore, the matter about which anyone proposes to write will be either fresh or it will have been treated beforehand by another poet. If the matter has been treated earlier, the contemporary author will have to follow the pattern of the established poetic treatment; but certain collateral matters not affecting the principal theme—such as comparisons, flagrant poetic license, vague syntactic relationships, and practices affecting quantities and syllables—need not be followed. **4.** This is not because the use of comparisons ought to be completely abandoned, but, rather, modern authors should use them sparingly; one will be able to do this, since a trope produces a figurative turn of speech without resorting to such devices. Consequently, "this work will not discuss them" (Hor., *Poet.*, 19). **5.** It was indeed incumbent upon ancient authors to expand their material with digressions and other matter only slightly related to their topic, so that their sparse material, then abounding in poetic figures, might swell into an artificial luxuriance. This practice, however, is not allowed modern authors; for new advances put an end to old practices. **6.** Furthermore, we ought not to imitate flagrant examples of poetic license in the quantities of syllables. For these abuses certainly should not be allowed to drive out truth or analogy "simply because the desire is reason enough" (Juv., *Sat.*, VI, 223). What is accounted a fault to us was accorded to the ancients as a grace. No irregularity in versification is permitted modern authors except these two: all may lengthen the syllable at the penthemimeral caesura, and those most advanced in prosody may practice caesural elision. **7.** Vague syntactic relationships ought to be eliminated from modern practice. It is, however, permissible to introduce them as quotations from older authors, as in Virgil's *Aeneid,* for example:

> Pars arduus altis
> Pulverulentus equis furit. (*Aen.*, VII, 625)
> (Some erect on high steeds and stirring up dust rage.)

This same fault is found in Statius:

> Haec manus Adrastum numero ter mille secuti. (*Theb.* IV, 63)
> (This troop, three-thousand strcng, which follows Adrastus.)

Here this figure is double because of the gender and the number.[53] **8.** One ought to avoid improper word usage[54] such as is found in Virgil's *Bucolics:*

> Ardebat Alexim. (*Ecl.*, II, 1)
> (He burned with passion Alexis-wise.)

Or in Statius:

> Ceu Flegrae fessus anhelat proelia. (*Theb.*, XI, 7)
> (Breathless, he pants as if at Phlegra's battle.)

There are endless abuses of this sort which ought to be closely attended to but not extended. In this matter it behooves moderns more to apologize for the ancients than to imitate them. Indeed:

> Even today children feel what their elders regret.

9. Thus in any discussion of human speech three areas occur or commend themselves to our attention: art, error, and figures. We ought to imitate art, fault ought to be eliminated, and figures indeed ought to be restrained.

10. Furthermore, one ought to be wary of the idle use of words and sentiments. Here is an example of the idle use of words, "They were going where they could; they were not going where they could not go."[55] This sentence is an example of *perissologia* or the superfluous use of many words. *Pleonasmus* or the superfluous use of only one word is exemplified in Virgil: "Orally she spoke thus" (*Aen.,* I, 614), or in Lucan's "Thus did that Jupiter admonish."[56] It appears that the "that" of the quotation from Lucan is superfluous. *Tautologia* is the superfluous repetition of words, although the repetition of words and often of sentiments may be fitting rather than superfluous. Superfluity of sentiments is technically called *macrologia,* that is, longwindedness which says nothing necessary. **11.** It should be noted that fitting repetition may be used for three reasons: for the sake of exposition, for the sake of greater vividness, and for the sake of addition. An addition may be either expository words or vivid sentiments. In both cases an expression is repeated so that something is added, as in Statius:

> Astur, the most handsome,
> Astur, relying on his horse.[57]

An idea may be repeated so that it can be explained, as Lucan does when speaking of Caesar and Pompey:

> The fields of Hesperia burn from savage plunderings. (*Phars.,* II,
> 534)

In the next line he repeats the idea, so that he might make clear who the savage plunderers are:

> The fury of Gaul is pouring over the snowy Alps. (*Phars.,* II, 535)

A word may be repeated for the sake of vividness as in Statius:

> To arms, Tydeus, to arms, men. (*Theb.,* III, 348)

An idea may be deliberately repeated as in this intercalaric verse or refrain in the *Bucolics:*

> Bring Daphnis home from town, my songs, bring him back. (Virg.,
> *Ecl.,* VIII, 84)

12. There are many other faults which ought to be avoided in the execution of the matter, such as *acirologia,* that is, the improper use of words, as seen in Statius speaking of Tydeus:

> Nor can he look forward to death. (*Theb.,* II, 607)

that is, "fear"; for one looks forward to the good and fears the bad. Another fault is *amphibologia,* that is, an ambiguous construction such as:

> Crossing the Halys, Croesus will lay waste a mighty kingdom.[58]

There are other faults such as *cacephaton,*[59] that is, blurred speech such as:

> Arrige(s) aures, (o) Pamphyle. (Ter., *And.,* V, 4, 30)
> (You, perk up your ears, Pamphilus.)

There are still others such as *eclipsis, tapinosis, cacosyntheton,*[60] and many more. If some want to imitate these for themselves, let them consult the *Barbarismus.*[61] The occurrence of the faults discussed above is to be attributed, not to the ignorance of the poets, but to poetic license. for these poets who employed figures for the sake of variety to take away distasteful tedium were not inexperienced but imaginative.

13. Up to now I have discussed how superfluous language ought to be eliminated. What follows concerns how words ought not be needlessly supplied. For instance, in human actions there is a certain usual succession. For certain actions are preludes to others and certain ones are consequences of others. For instance, in the usual course of love[62] seeing comes first, then follow desire, approach, conversation, blandishments, and finally the hoped for union of the two. For we have the testimony of Ovid:

> What two wish seldom fails to happen. (*Am.,* II, 3, 16)

Ovid, moreover, affirms that such action has stages, saying:

> These things will come in turn and by degree. (*Ars,* I, 482)

Similarly, in the execution of the material we ought certainly to copy the steps of the action straightforwardly, so that there is no interruption of the account just as there was none in the actions mentioned above. Ovid, however, seems to interrupt or telescope the order of the action where, speaking of the Inachian maid, he says:

> Jupiter had seen Io returning from her father's river
> And he said, "O maiden worthy of Jupiter and
> Destined to make some man happy on your marriage bed, etc."
> (*Met.,* I, 588)

The coherence of the account is interrupted, for two steps are omitted: desire and approach. In addition, the sighting and the conversation are connected as though they were in the normal order. But as Ovid said in his last work:

> I would have corrected these things had it been permitted. (*Tr.,* I, 7, 40)

14. The next section discusses how awkward elements in previously treated material may be turned into something better. For ex-

ample, in the execution of material previously treated some problems
may occur because this material is somewhat confused and obscure
and is not handled with enough artfulness, as in Ovid's account of the
murder of Argos where it is said:

> It remained to tell his words. (*Met.,* I, 700)

and in the rest of his account up to the words:

> About to tell such things. (*Met.,* I, 713)

Lest a similar confusion should occur, one must alter the material. One
should keep an equivalent meaning but make the manner of expression
better so that statements which the poet has wrapped in an envelope of
confusion may be made lucid through a clear but equivalent statement.
15. Therefore, modern authors will have to concern themselves with
equivalent statements in traditional materials, changing words and expressions. Otherwise, anyone wishing to appropriate for his own use
the original words and constructions might be assumed to want good
sense.

   16. Up to now we have considered previously handled material,
that is, poetic stories which naked Hottentots[63] plough through in
school exercises in versification. What follows concerns fresh material,
the treatment of which must above all follow custom, so that with the
proper use of words we may describe actions as they usually are. We
must make sure that the expressive execution of the material is seen as
conforming to the subject being treated, that is, so that what we hear
corresponds to the common understanding. **17.** Either the attributes
of a person or those of a thing will be involved. **18.** If the attributes of
a person are involved, let the person be set forth in a description in
which he is so clearly seen on the basis of the imaginative description
or of the report that his character is made clear with the aid of words.
For example:

> Choose a girl to whom you may say, "You alone are pleasing to
>   me." (Ovid., *Ars,* I, 41)

And such a one will be pleasing to you having been so described in your
statement. Approval is expressed in this way. For the purpose of censure let her be described as so hideous that she makes herself repugnant in your eyes and in those of all mankind. **19.** If the attributes of a
thing are involved, the description ought to follow the general ideas of
mankind and the authority of custom. In describing the attributes of a
thing, moreover, more brevity and restraint of speech ought to be
employed than in describing the attributes of a person, so that the
material may be made clear in a sentence unless stylistic grace sup-
plements meaning as by quotations, metaphors, epithets, and similes.

Indeed, since Boethius says contraries harmonize with contraries,[64] whatever treatment displeases ought to be omitted; similarly, the beauty of the idea ought to be developed fully.

20. At this point much remains to be said about the execution of the matter but, since our chariot sighs for the goalpost and lest we run the risk of boredom, what follows deals with changes in the material, and this certainly relates to its execution. Change in material may be twofold: one is a change of words and meanings with an equivalent sense retained; the other is a change of words only and not of meanings.[65]

21. A change in meanings and words may be accomplished by the use of *periphrasis. Periphrasis* is circumlocution. This trope may be executed in two ways: either the bare truth may be embellished with ornamentation or the foulness of an idea may be avoided by a roundabout statement. The truth is set forth ornately in Virgil:

> And now Aurora leaving early the saffron bed of
> Tithonus was sprinkling earth with her fresh rays. (*Aen.*, IV, 584)

The sense is "now day was breaking." An example of my own follows:

> Learning is the companion of experience; random teaching
> Profits no one; continued instruction strengthens the student.

The sense of this is simply: "experience is the best teacher." Again there may be *periphrasis* when the foul is avoided by roundabout statement as in Virgil:

> He sought rest,
> Sinking on the bosom of his mate. (*Aen.*, VIII, 406)

Or thus:

> The paramour smiles at her suitor for his gifts. Love
> Eager for favor gains admittance between modesty's gates.

In each example intercourse is suggested in decent terms. **22.** Further, another change in words and meanings, but with an equivalent sense retained, is effected when active constructions are turned into passive ones or vice versa, as in this manner:

> Love torments the gods above; even the gods are tormented by
> love.
> Knowledge fashions the youth; the youth is fashioned by
> knowledge.

23. All transitive constructions are able to be reversed in this manner. Further, words and meanings are changed in another way when a simple or partial notion is expanded by sentences or clauses. Thus for the partial notion "she blushes" one may write, "a blush reddens her face," or for "he mourns" one may say, "he floods his face with tears," or for "he grows angry" one may write "a menacing wrath spreads across his countenance." Other modes of expressions may be substituted in a similar way so long as they serve to flesh out the ideas treated.

24. The following concerns changes in words but not in meaning; synonyms are often necessary for this. The meaning of synonyms is the same but with a different connotation, thus one synonym can often be substituted for another. Nor is it idle to say "often." For many synonyms, on account of their diverse connotations, are not mutually interchangeable; on the other hand, the connotation of one word may often replace that of another, as in this example:

> Hair may become tresses, waves billows, or the wind a breeze.
> The crops become a harvest and a house lodgings.

If, on the other hand, the connotations of words differ widely, one may not be substituted for the other without doing violence to the original meaning. **25.** Thus in this connection it is important that the versifier be practiced in the accepted denotations and connotations of words, since speech is judged favorable on the basis of these two. For ignorance of the meaning of words is harmful, leading to other stumblings to learning of which there are these ten: wrapping ideas in obscure brevity (as Horace said:

> I labor to be brief
> And become obscure.) (*Poet.,* 25);

digressing into superfluous loquacity; worrying over. accepted language; wandering because of a doubtful mind; an overly scrupulous concern with meaning; boundless confusion of speech; a barren waste of talent; an unseemly hastening into linguistic disasters; a confused agitation over words; overlooking the meaning of expressions. **26.** As a remedy for stumbling blocks of this sort, particularly in the graceful marriage of words, we ought to follow usage:

> In whose hands lie the judgment, right, and rule of speech. (Hor.,
>   *Poet.,* 72)

For expressions are but the handmaidens and tribute payers of usage, to whom they yield as if to the will of a paterfamilias. Hence, since the authority of analogy with usage is so strong, no one may presume to stray beyond the license and permission of usage. Indeed language is ordained so properly that only within the limits of such propriety can a verse seem to be fittingly playful. **27.** Further, one expression will be able to be used in the place of another even though its meaning is logically antecedent to the other, as in Statius:

> Sure of his death, Oenides passes him by; too proud to take spoil.
> (*Theb.,* VIII, 588)

"Too proud" means "he disdained," pride is certainly logically antecedent to "disdaining." **28.** It is similar when the meanings of expressions have a mutual range, as in Horace's "to admire nothing," that is, "to desire nothing." **29.** It is similar when what pertains to a person is attributed to a property of a person as in Lucan:

> Every power will be impatient of a sharer. (*Phars.,* I, 93)

Here "power" means "powerful man." **30.** Or when that which is caused is attributed to the cause, as in Virgil:

> I remember that I prolonged long suns with singing, (*Ecl.,* IX, 52)

that is, "days." For the sun is the efficient cause of the day. **31.** Again, a change in words may be effected by many other means, as when expressions have collateral or associated meanings or when we use *synecdoche* or *metaphor.*

32. What follows concerns correction. Correction is, insofar as it is accepted, an examination of metrical verse, removing blemishes, and setting forth graceful emendations. In this process three things relate to the pupil and two to the corrector, namely these: marking faults and showing a remedy. In these two functions no other ordering ought to be observed. **33.** For the marking of faults to be avoided comes first, and the showing of graceful expression to be chosen follows. Indeed, the elimination of faults comes first; otherwise any edifying graceful expression which follows will be in vain, as Horace says:

> Unless a vessel is clean, whatever you pour in sours. (*Ep.,* I, 2, 54)

Even though the criticism of verse has been explained in many places above, nevertheless, certain things remain to be discussed in the following passages. **34.** In verses that are separate and distinct sentences the correction ought to proceed along the lines of *zeugma* or *hypozeuxis.* I prefer the idea never or rarely to be completed in one line unless it be a proverb. In particular, the idea of a hexameter ought to extend into the pentameter, or the clauses of a pentameter ought to begin in the hexameter. In fact, the hexameter and the pentameter perform a joint and indivisible function, for the pentameter ought to serve and wait upon the hexameter, either by explaining or concluding its idea. For it is fitting that those who share a function should accompany one another in sentences. **35.** Not all blemishes included in a poem, however, can be corrected by a teacher, for according to Ovid:

It does not always lie in the doctor's power to cure a sickness.
Now and then the illness is stronger than learned skill. (*Pont.,* I, 3,
17)

"Hence someone who is not fit today will be less so tomorrow" (Ovid,
Rem., 94) unless practice is insisted upon in the daily passage of time.
Do not let the arrogance of ignorance produce real harm; do not let the
spark of a disease burst into a bonfire. Indeed:

Too late is a cure attempted
When through long delays the malady is grown strong. (Ovid,
Rem., 92)

36. Ovid, moreover, testifies to the power of habit, saying:

A dribble hollows out the rock (unless it does not always fall).
(*Pont.,* IV, 10, 5)

And elsewhere Ovid says:

Nothing is stronger than habit. (*Ars,* II, 3, 45)

And again:

With difficulty is habit forgotten. (*Rem.,* 503)

Even though nature may be lavish with talent, habit nevertheless
develops it; and just as practice makes it strong, perseverance crowns
it. **37.** Further, carrying over the idea to a third line is not to be done,
so that a long carry-over of words may be avoided.

38. Further, a monosyllabic word should never be the final word
in a line, lest as in Horace's words, from a mountain swelling up into a
huge size at last:

A ridiculous mouse is born. (*Poet.,* 139)

Nor should a wine jar end up as a small pitcher. As Horace says:

That began to be molded as a wine jar, why as
The wheel turned did it wind up as a small pitcher? (*Poet.,* 21)

39. A pentameter should always end in a disyllabic word except when
this is impossible. **40.** In addition one should always pay close attention to the grace of recitation and to the distinctness of separate
sentences. For how something is said is often of more value than what
is said:

And whatever you recite badly ends up as your work. (Mart., *Ep.,*
I, 38, 2)

41. At this point many instructions about correction remain to be
given. But since judgments on verses are aired everywhere above, we

must drive on to the next subject lest I seem to "fly in circles through that same air" (Ovid, *Met.,* II, 721); for to no good reason should diligent listeners test their hearing rather than their writing. As Horace says:

> What comes through the ears stirs the mind more slowly
> That what is entrusted to faithful eyes. (*Poet.,* 180)

42. Certain untrained persons usurp the role of a corrector and, like the blind leading the blind, fall into a pit with their disciples; such a one is Rufus. But in a kingdom of blind men a one-eyed man is king, and he holds sway over the people who trust him. And they are corrupted along with the corrupt leader, they grow red with shame along with the redheaded one, and they become blind companions of a blind man.

43. The following concerns those three areas which pertain to the student, namely: confession of error, not hiding behind excuses, and accepting blame. Confession of error leads to forgiveness, not hiding behind excuses avoids pride, accepting blame augurs well for improvement. One ought not hide behind excuses lest one's fault be deflected toward the innocent. For sometimes the guilt of an offender spills over onto the head of an innocent person. Nevertheless, an error will often be forgiven if its occurrence is not frequent. For:

> If Jupiter unleashed his thunderbolt each time
> Men sinned, then he would be alone in a short time. (Ovid, *Tr.,* II,
> 33)

44. Those for whom error is a daily affair and who need a curb more than spurs ought to be severely upbraided often lest the silence of the teacher be taken as a form of approval. For when error goes unreproved, more error is bred. The corrector must be very careful in this area, for we have Ovid's testimony that:

> This work is harder than writing. (*Pont.,* I, 5, 17)

45. Further, we must not overlook what Horace says about the examination of verse, that is, that the words are broken up, as it were, by the reading of the poem; and if they have pleased being considered as prose and have exhibited a graceful marriage of words, they will be more pleasing by far set in verse. Horace says in his book of *Satires:*[66]

> It is not enough to sketch out a line in simple words,
> So that if you should break it up, any father whatever
> Would fume in the same way as the actor. (*Sat.,* I, 4, 54)

46. Further, the following is another instruction concerning correction that Horace, speaking in his second book of *Epistles,* gives:

> But one who wishes to make a correct poem
> Will employ the spirit of an honest censor as well as
> His tablets; he will dare wherever words are
> Lackluster or empty or are esteemed unworthy
> To remove them even though they be reluctant to go. (*Ep.*, II, 2,
>   107)

And a little later he says:

> He will pour out wealth and bless Latium with rich speech;
> He will cut back that which is too luxuriant and with
> Sensible refinement smooth that which is too rough,
> And do away with that which lacks forcefulness. (*Ep.*, II, 2, 121)

47. Further, let all deeds that relate to the color red be interpreted in a figurative manner. Since the iniquity of the color red is most abundant in Rufus and will probably shine forth in a follower of his, let whatever is said about Rufus or Redheads be understood figuratively as referring to Arnulf of Saint-Evurce,[67] who daily provokes me with abuse even though I am not around him. I think his tongue is poisoned with the venom of envy. Alas, Redhead, whatever you presume to crow about me, "no distinction will ever make you worthy of the wrath of Caesar" (Luc., *Phars.*, III, 137). It is hard to kick against the pricks;[68] to be sure, he who often kicks back against the pricks inflicts upon himself the punishment of those two sharp points. **48.** Although I have meted out the punishment you so richly deserve very sparingly in this little work, I shall do it quite fully in an exchange of letters since:

> You think nothing is safer than
> To attack me at my age.

Let a slanderous tongue not be imputed to me, if I only slander a slanderer. I take comfort in Solomon's words: "Answer a fool according to his folly, lest you be thought like him."[69] Therefore, having been injured by your attacks:

> I bite a biter back;[70] oppressed I oppress; wounded
> I wound; tit for tat is only fair,

so that your iniquity, kept alive by my efforts, cannot be buried in the ashes of oblivion:

> It shames you, Rufus, that I proclaim your scarlet sins,
> But I shall shine forth even though reluctantly.
> "Rufus, you are broken up," I'll cry when your sides burst.[71]
> Whatever I try to say will turn out poetry.[72]
> When you meet Thaïs, you alone quiver with ecstasy,   5
> You alone feel love, thinking her yours alone. She is not.
> You each grow red with the same passion; scarlet woman
> And red-haired man couple like he-goat and she-goat.

As the female ape submits to her mate, so does your wench.
Greedy Rufus, you would turn to usury with a ready hand;
You return to the law of Otho and to the well of a sot.[73]   10

49. I have already discussed the twofold manner of beginning a work, that is, *zeugma* and *hypozeuxis,* as well as using general sentiments or proverbs. I have also discussed not mixing verb tenses, the method of writing, the attributes of a person or an action, the threefold elegance of versification, the figures and tropes, the execution of material, the changes in material, and the corrections; thus what follows concerns the conclusion. Thus this work is concluded with a happy conclusion. A conclusion, as the term is used here, is an appropriate ending of a poem that completes its overall design. **50.** Conclusions vary greatly among different authors. For the conclusion may be an epilogue, that is, a recapitulation of ideas, as in the first fable of Avianus, when he says:

Let anyone who has thought woman faithful consider these verses
Directed to him and realize that he is meant in this poem. (*Fab.,* I,
16)

A conclusion might, on the other hand, be effected through an emendation of the work, as in Statius's *Thebaid:*

This will perish, yet due honors will be paid me. (*Theb.,* XII, 819)

Again, a conclusion may often be a plea for indulgence, as in Ovid:

I would have corrected these things had it been permitted. (*Tr.,* I,
7, 40)

Again, a conclusion may be made through a display of boasting as in Ovid's *Remedies:*

You men and women alike who have been healed by my poem
Before long will be returning grateful vows to a holy poet. (*Rem.,*
814)

In addition, a conclusion may be written before the author intends by those authors whose deaths occur before they finish their work; in such cases this ought to be called an ending instead of a conclusion; an example is Lucan's:

He beseiged Magnus who stormed his very walls. (*Phars.,* X, 546)

Also, a conclusion may be an expression of gratitude, as in the *Bucolics:*

That I have sung as your poet, O Muses, will be enough. (Virg.,
Ecl., X, 70)

Here Virgil is seen to show gratitude to the Muses, since he says "your" poet. **51.** A conclusion ought to be introduced in this way, just as this work ends in praise of God from Whose fountainhead the streams of this work have flowed. It is fitting that I attribute to Him Whose legate I now am and Whose legatee I wish to be, to the One Who shares my work and my attainments whatever beauty in this work may have impressed the reader.

> O Christ, honor and glory be Thine Who rule with the Father,
> King with King, God with God, world without end."Thou art
> Equal to the Father, one Being; not the same
> As the Father, not different from the Father.
> Both the Father and the Son and the Spirit are God.   5
> A Unity, not one; a Trinity, not three; three and yet the same."
>   (Matt., *Tob.*, 2081–84)
> No difference of nature divides the unity, one Whole
> In three parts, the unity overcomes the triplicity.
> I give thanks as vessel to potter, work to workman,
> Servant to king, creature to Creator, as son to father.   10
> Thou guidest me to speak, to steer life's course, Oh Pilot,
> That leadest me into the glorious haven of rest.
> No tongue can describe nor any wisdom know Thee
> Whose spaciousness no space can contain.
> Thy goodness is of such a nature and so boundless   15
> That it makes deceivers of our most gracious words.
> Thou art a day without clouds, the all in all,
> The whole without parts; Thou art power almighty.
> Discernment discerns Thee not, and ignorance ignores Thee
> Whom the tongues of men are fearful of describing.   20
> Space stands in awe of Thee as vaster and Thou awest
> Eternity as yet young, end of endings, beginning of beginnings.
> Unmoved Thou movest all; Thou art triune and yet single,
> Art three and one; let one honor be paid to three.
> Eye does not see Thee nor does ear hear Thee nor   25
> Reason perceive Thee whom gracious faith reveals.
> I hasten my steps toward Paris; farewell, Orléans,
> So pleasant to me a student there in the days of Primas.
> This little book instructs boys about verses; it takes
> Its name from that fact; it can teach the major ideas.   30
> Farewell, I pray, and fear not the stings of envy,
> Little book written during the course of two months.
> I recall what is pleasant to have recalled; "the meadows
> Have drunk enough" (Virg., *Ecl.*, III,111). Here ends
> Vendôme's completed work.

And if anything shall have been left over, let it be consumed by fire, that is, committed to the Holy Spirit. Amen.

A P P E N D I X

The twenty-nine rhetorical colors that Matthew lists in III, 47, are defined below:

Repetitio: repetition of a word or phrase at the beginning of a number of verses

Conversio: repetition of a word or phrase at the end of a number of verses

Complexio: repetition of one word or phrase at the beginning of a number of verses and of another word at the end of these verses

Traductio: repetition of a word in a different grammatical form

Contentio: contrasting ideas in adjacent phrases

Exclamatio: an exclamation

Ratiocinatio: a rhetorical question

Sententia: an epigrammatic expression, a maxim

Contrarium: a statement of an idea by denying its contrary before the idea is stated affirmatively

Membrum orationis or *articulus:* emphasizing an idea by expressing it in a series of parallel phrases, usually without conjunctions

Similiter cadens: two or more words of the same case whose case endings rhyme

Similiter desinens: two or more indeclinable words that rhyme

Commixtio: mixing of styles, ideas, or grammatical categories

Annominatio: bringing together or contrasting words similar in sound, but different in meaning

Subjectio: answering a question one has just asked in order to anticipate objections

Gradatio: repeating the final word of one clause as the initial word of the next throughout a series

Diffinitio: a brief definition of a word or a phrase

Transitio: a transition from one point to another by a brief summary of what has been said and a suggestion of what will be said next

Correptio: retracting what has been said in order to replace it with a more fitting expression; the usual term is *correctio*

Occupatio: bringing up something by asserting that it will not be mentioned

Disjunctio: grammatically parallel clauses ending in verbs whose meanings contrast

Conjunctum: two clauses connected by a single verb placed between them, *zeugma* in the middle

Adjunctum: a type of *zeugma* in which two clauses have a single verb that comes either at the beginning of the first clause or the end of the last clause

Conduplicatio: repetition of a word or phrase for emphasis

Commutatio: inverting the word order of one clause in the following one, so that a contradictory idea is expressed, using *chiasmus* to express contrast; for example, eat to live, not live to eat

Dubitatio: hesitation, expressing doubt over word choice

Dissolutio: *asyndeton,* a series of words or clauses without connecting conjunctions

Praecisio: a sentence that breaks off abruptly and hints at an idea rather than expressing it openly, *aposiopesis*

Conclusio: a brief summary setting forth what necessarily follows from what has been said, peroration

N O T E S

1. English translations of these are in the Loeb Classical Library: Horace, *Satires, Epistles, Ars Poetica,* trans. H. Rushton Fairclough (Cambridge, Mass., and London, 1966); Cicero, *De inventione,* trans. H. M. Hubbell (New York and London, 1936); *Rhetorica ad Herennium,* trans. Harry Caplan (Cambridge, Mass., and London, 1968).

2. There is an English translation of Cassiodorus: Cassiodorus Senator, *An Introduction to Divine and Human Readings,* trans. Leslie Webber Jones (New York, 1946). The standard editions of the others are Isidore, *Isidori Hispalensis Etymologiarum sive originum libri XX,* ed. Wallace M. Lindsay (Oxford, 1911) and Martianus Capella, *De nuptiis Philologiae et Mercurii,* ed. Wilhelm A. Dick (Leipzig, 1925).

3. The texts of these grammarians are in *Grammatici Latini,* ed. Heinrich Keil, 7 vols. (Leipzig, 1857–1880).

4. Bede's work has been translated by Gussie Hecht Tanenhaus, "Bede's *De schematibus et tropis*—A Translation," *Quarterly Journal of Speech,* XLVIII (1962), 237–53. For English translations of representative arts of preaching and of letter writing see *Three Medieval Rhetorical Arts,* ed. James J. Murphy (Berkeley, Los Angeles, and London, 1971). For a general survey of the various arts see Ernst R. Curtius, *European Literature and the Latin Middle Ages,* trans. Willard R. Trask, Bollingen Series 36 (New York, 1953), pp. 39–45, 75–76, 148–154. For more detailed studies see the following: Edmond Faral, *Les Arts poétiques du XII*^e *et du XIII*^e *siècle* (Paris, 1924; repr. 1962) and James J. Murphy, *Rhetoric in the Middle Ages* (Berkeley, 1974); for the grammatical arts see Robert H. Robbins, *Ancient and Medieval Grammatical Theory in Europe* (London, 1951) and Charles Thurot, "Notices et extraits de divers manuscrits latins pour servir à l'histoire des doctrines grammaticles au moyen âge," *Notices et extraits,* XXII (1868), 1–592 (repr. Frankfurt-am-Main, 1964); for arts of preaching see Harry Caplan, "Classical Rhetoric and the Mediaeval Theory of Preaching," *Classical Philology,* XXVIII (1933), 73–96 and Th.-M. Charland, *Artes praedicandi: contribution à l'histoire de la rhetorique au moyen âge,* Publications de l'institut d'études médiévales d'Ottawa 7 (Paris and Ottawa, 1936); for arts of letter writing see Noel Denholm-Young, "The *Cursus* in England," *Collected Papers of N. Denholm-Young* (Cardiff, 1969), pp. 42–73 [This was first published in *Oxford Essays in Medieval History Presented to Herbert Edward Salter* (Oxford, 1934), pp. 68–103.] and Charles H. Haskins, "The Early *Artes dictandi* in Italy," *Studies in Mediaeval Culture* (Oxford, 1929), pp. 170–92.

5. The Latin is "Dictaminum . . . tria sunt genera a veteribus diffinita, prosaicum, ut Cassiodori, metricum, ut Virgilii, et rithmicum, ut Primatis,"

Die Ars dictandi des Thomas von Capua, ed. Emmy Heller (Heidelberg, 1929), p. 13.

6. Charles S. Baldwin, *Medieval Rhetoric and Poetic* (New York, 1928; repr. 1959), p. 110.

7. Marbod's treatise is in J. P. Migne, *Patrologia Latina,* CLXXI, 1687–1692; Geoffrey's *Summa* is in Faral, *Arts poétiques,* pp. 321–27.

8. Faral also prints the text to the *Laborintus* of Eberhard the German. He includes brief analyses of two other arts of poetry, the *Ars versificaria* of Gervase of Melkley and the *Poetria* of John of Garland. For the text of Gervase see Gervais van Melkley, *Ars poetica,* ed. Hans-Jurgen Grabener, *Forschungen zur romanischen Philologie,* XVII (Münster, 1965). John's *Poetria* is the *De Arte prosayca metrica et rithmica,* which, as the title suggests, treats all three forms of discourse: prose, metrical verse, and rhythmical verse. Giovanni Mari published the sections on prose and metrical verse in *Romanische Forschungen,* XIII (1902), 885–950, and the section on rhythmical verse in *Il tratti medievali di rithmica latina* (Milan, 1899). The *Ars versificatoria* has been translated by Ernest Gallo, "Matthew of Vendôme: Introductory Treatise on the Art of Poetry," *Proceedings of the American Philosophical Society,* CXVIII, No. 1 (1974), 51–92; Gallo summarizes Parts II and III rather than translating them completely. The *Poetria nova* has been translated by Margaret F. Nims (Toronto, 1967); Jane Baltzell Kopp in Murphy, *Rhetorical Arts,* pp. 27–108; and Ernest Gallo, *The Poetria Nova and Its Sources in Early Rhetorical Doctrine* (The Hague and Paris, 1971). Gallo's translation has the Faral text on facing pages. Geoffrey's *Documentum* has been translated by Roger Parr (Milwaukee, 1968). For an English version of the prose and metrical sections of John's work see *The Parisiana Poetria of John of Garland,* ed. and trans. Traugott Lawler (New Haven, 1974).

9. Faral, *Arts poétiques,* pp. 2, 4. Frederic J. E. Raby, *A History of Secular Latin Poetry in the Middle Ages,* 2nd ed. (Oxford, 1957), II, 30; Douglas Kelly, "The Scope of the Treatment of Composition in the Twelfth- and Thirteenth-Century Arts of Poetry," *Speculum,* XLI (1966), 262, 269.

10. Faral, *Arts poétiques,* p. 107.

11. Max Manitius, *Geschichte der lateinischen Literatur des Mittelalters,* (Munich, 1931), III, 741. This is also the view of Robert R. Bolgar, *The Classical Heritage and Its Beneficiaries* (Cambridge, England, 1963), who writes, "His first book [Part I of the *Art*] is largely devoted to hints on how to invent subject matter" (p. 211).

12. See Kelly, "Scope of Treatment," p. 263, n. 11, and Hennig Brinkmann, *Zu Wesen und Form mittelalterlicher Dichtung* (Halle, 1928), p. 44.

13. Faral, *Arts poétiques,* p. 76.

14. Matthew somewhat idiosyncratically discusses antithesis as a trope. Isidore lists it among the figures (*Etym.,* I, 36, 21); Donatus does not discuss it as either. Harry Caplan, trans., *Ad Herennium,* notes, "The ancient rhetoricians differ widely, some regarding Antithesis as a figure of diction, others as a figure of thought, and still others as belonging to both classes" (p. 376, n. a). The *Ad Herennium* treats antithesis as a figure of diction (IV, 15, 21) and a figure of thought (IV, 45, 58). Matthew shares this confusion, for he lists *contentio* (antithesis) among the rhetorical colors (III, 47).

15. Matthew does not discuss these figures: *prolepsis* (anticipation), *syllepsis* (a single word modifying or governing two or more words though it agrees

with only one), *homoeoptoton* (use of words with the same inflectional endings that rhyme), and *hirmos* (periodic sentence). He does not discuss these tropes: *catachresis* (improper or unnatural use of a word), *antonomasia* (use of an epithet in place of a proper name), *hyperbaton* (transposition of words into an unnatural order), *hyperbole, homoeosis* (resemblance), and *onomatopoeia*.

16. For Donatus see Keil, *Grammatici Latini,* IV, 397–402; for Isidore see *Etymologies,* I, 36–37.

17. Marbod's treatise is in Migne, *Patrologia Latina,* CLXXI, 1687–1692. See Kelly, "Scope of Treatment," p. 266 and Faral, *Arts poétiques,* p. 52. Marbod's work was a popular elementary textbook: Jean de Ghellinck, *L'Essor de la littérature latine au XIIe siècle* (Brussels and Paris, 1946), II, 239–40.

18. See Kelly, "Scope of Treatment," pp. 261–62.

19. For a description of Bernard's method see John of Salisbury, *The Metalogicon,* trans. Daniel D. McGarry (Berkeley and Los Angeles, 1962), pp. 66–70.

20. For Eberhard's discussion of ways of beginning see Faral, *Arts poétiques,* pp. 346–47; for Geoffrey's treatment see *Poetria nova,* lines 87–154, and *Documentum,* Pt. I; for John's remarks see *Romanische Forschungen,* XIII (1902), 905–7.

21. I have translated *sententiae* as "meaning" throughout this section. Ernest Gallo, "Matthew of Vendôme: Introductory Treatise," writes, "Sententiae: the meaning in this context is quite certainly "sentences" and not "meanings" (p. 87, n. 77). Nowhere else does Matthew use the word in this sense. My reading, puzzling as it is, is supported by James J. Murphy who summarizes the section thus, "There are two methods of permutation: changing the words but not the sense, and changing both the words and the sense" (*Rhetoric in the Middle Ages,* p. 167).

22. See Faral, *Arts poétiques,* pp. 89–97.

23. Ibid., p. 97.

24. Kelly, "Scope of Treatment," pp. 261–62.

25. Raby, *Secular Latin Poetry,* II, 35.

26. Baldwin, *Medieval Rhetoric,* pp. 186, 187.

27. Curtius, *European Literature,* p. 414.

28. For sources of Matthew and other late medieval theoreticians see Murphy, *Rhetoric in the Middle Ages,* pp. 3–132, Gallo, *Poetria Nova,* pp. 133–231, and Faral, *Arts poétiques,* pp. 99–103.

29. Curtius, *European Literature,* p. 153.

30. Murphy, *Rhetorical Arts,* p. 30.

31. Arnulf was a colleague of Matthew's at Orléans; he is known to have written commentaries on Ovid and Lucan. See Arnulf of Orléans, *Glosule super Lucanum,* ed. Berthe M. Marti, American Academy in Rome, *Papers and Monographs,* XVIII (Rome, 1958), xviii–xxii for a discussion of Matthew's relations with Arnulf; also Leopold Delisle, "Les Ecoles d'Orléans au XIIe et XIIIe siècle," *Annuaire-Bulletin de la Société de l'Histoire de France* (1869), p. 1339, and Emile Lesne, *Les Ecoles de la fin du VIIIe siècle à la fin du XIIe* in *Histoire de le propriété ecclésiastique en France,* (Lille, 1940), V, 177, n. 6, and 185.

32. Barthélemy Hauréau, rev. of L. Bourgain, *Mattaei Vindocinensis Ars Versificatoria,* (Thesim proponebat facultati litterarum Parisiensi) *Journal des Savants* (April 1883), p. 212.

33. Philip S. Allen, *Medieval Latin Lyrics* (Chicago, 1931), p. 250.

34. Curtius, *European Literature,* p. 50; he quotes Martin Schanz, *Geschichte der romanischen Literatur,* IV, No. 2 (Munich, 1920), 77.

35. Walter B. Sedgwick, "The Style and Vocabulary of the Latin Arts of Poetry of the Twelfth and Thirteenth Centuries," *Speculum,* III (1928), 353.

36. Faral, *Arts poétiques,* p. 78.

37. Baldwin, *Medieval Rhetoric,* p. 186.

38. See Curtius, *European Literature,* pp. 487–94.

39. Brinkmann, *Zu Wesen und Form,* p. 63.

40. Curtius, *European Literature,* pp. 193–94.

41. See IV, 51, 27–28. For biography see Faral, *Arts poétiques,* pp. 1–3. The biographical passages from Matthew's other poems are printed by Faral, p. 1, n. 3 and p. 2, n. 5. See also Manitius, *Geschichte,* III, 737–39.

42. For the text of the *Poetic Epistles* see "Ein poetischer Briefsteller von Matthäus von Vendôme," ed. Wilhelm Wattenbach, *Sitzungsberichte der philosophisch-philologischen und historischen Klasse der koeniglichen bayerischen Akademie der Wissenschaften,* II (Munich, 1872), 570–631. For *Milo* see Gustave Cohen, ed., *La comédie latine en France au XIIe siècle,* (Paris, 1931), II, 168–77. *Pyramus and Thisbe* is printed in Paul Lehmann, *Pseudo-antike Literatur des Mittelalters)* Leipzig and Berlin, 1927), pp. 31–35. *Tobias* is edited by Friedrich A. W. Mueldener (Göttingen, 1855). For a discussion of the works mentioned by Matthew or others attributed to him see Faral, *Arts poétiques,* pp. 3–14; Manitius, *Geschichte,* III, 739–47, 1024–26; Raby, *Secular Latin Poetry,* II, 32–35; and Raby, *A History of Christian Latin Poetry from the Beginnings to the Close of the Middle Ages,* 2nd ed., (Oxford, 1953), pp. 304–5. The relevant passage from the *Poetic Epistles* is in Faral, *Arts poétiques,* p. 7.

43. In Faral, *Arts poétiques,* lines 663–64, 675–76.

44. See ibid., p. 35

45. Quoted in Hauréau, *Mattaei Vindocinensis,* p. 210.

46. Cited by Kelly, "Scope of Treatment," p. 263.

47. Quoted in Anders Gagner, *Florilegium Gallicum* (Lund, 1936), p. 11.

48. See Faral, *Arts poétiques,* p. 13.

49. *Proceedings of the British Academy,* XII (1926), 95–113. Manly's lecture is reprinted in Richard Schoeck and Jerome Taylor, *Chaucer Criticism: The Canterbury Tales* (Notre Dame, Ind., 1960), pp. 268–90. For an opinion that differs from Manly's see James J. Murphy, "A New Look at Chaucer and the Rhetoricians," *Review of English Studies,* n.s. 2, XV (1964), 1–20.

50. Faral, *Arts poétiques,* pp. 61–97, passim.

51. Curtius, *European Literature,* p. 76.

52. Ibid., p. 354.

53. Note these statements from Dante. "La bontade e la bellezza di ciascuno sermone sono intra loro partite e diverse; ché la bontade è ne la sentenza, e la bellezza è ne l'ornamento de la parole": The goodness and the beauty of each poem are separate and distinct, for its goodness is in its meaning and its beauty is in the ornament of the words (*Convivio,* II, 11). And "Si poesim recte consideremus; que nichil aliud est quam fictio rethorica musicaque poita": If we take the right view of poetry, which is nothing more than a fiction set forth rhetorically and musically (*De vulgari eloquentia,* II, 4). The quotations are from Dante Alighieri, *Opere minori,* ed. Alberto del Monte, 2nd ed. (Milan, 1966), pp. 314, 578.

54. C. S. Lewis, *The Discarded Image* (Cambridge, England, 1967), p. 175.

55. Raby, *Secular Latin Poetry,* II, 35.

56. Baldwin, *Medieval Rhetoric,* p. 187.

57. Helen Waddell, *The Wandering Scholars* (New York, 1961), p. 136.

58. Hauréau, *Mattaei Vindocinensis,* p. 207.

59. M.-D. Chenu, *Nature, Man, and Society in the Twelfth Century,* trans. Jerome Taylor and Lester K. Little (Chicago and London, 1968), pp. 118–19.

60. Winthrop Wetherbee, *Platonism and Poetry in the Twelfth Century* (Princeton, 1972), p. 148; see pp. 146–51 for a discussion of philosophical aspects of the *Ars versificatoria.*

61. Douglas Kelly, *Medieval Imagination* (Madison, Wisc., 1978), pp. 70–74, 84.

ART OF VERSIFICATION

1. Cf. Matth. 23:5.

2. Matthew often quotes from other writers without any acknowledgment. Faral has identified many of his quotations. Several of Matthew's unacknowledged quotations have been noted by Walter B. Sedgwick, "Notes and Emendations on Faral's *Les Arts poétiques,*" *Speculum,* II (1927), 332–36.

3. Cf. Ps. 21:6.

4. Matthew uses the color red to indicate fraud or malice. Sedgwick glosses the line: " 'In rufa pelle nemo latitat sine felle' (J. Werner, *Latein. Sprichworter . . . des Mittelalters* (Heidelberg: Winter, 1912), p. 41, Nr. 64): No one conceals himself in a red skin except to do ill" (Sedgwick, "Notes," p. 332).

5. Cf. Virgil, *Eclogues,* VII, 26.

6. Cf. Horace, *Art of Poetry,* 16.

7. Cf. Matth. 22:14.

8. It is not clear what Matthew means by four other ways of beginning that he rejects. In addition to *zeugma* and *hypozeuxis* he gives passing attention to *metonymy* as a way of beginning (I, 15) and considerable attention to beginning with a proverb (I, 16–29). Writing more than fifty years after Matthew, John of Garland recommends beginning with a proverb; an exemplum; a simile; a metaphor; an if, while, or since clause; or an ablative absolute (*Romanische Forschungen,* XII [1902], 905–7). The last four of John's methods of beginning are rhetorical or grammatical devices for starting the first sentence, as are *zeugma, hypozeuxis,* and *metonymy.* Perhaps some list such as John's was prevalent in Matthew's day, and he had reference to these other ways of starting the first sentence of a work.

9. Cf. Horace, *Satires,* I, 7.3.

10. Matthew frequently quotes from other works of his. I have indicated such quotations by using "Matt." plus the work quoted from. Many of Matthew's self-quotations are noted by Franco Munari, "Notrelle su Matteo di Vendôme," *Lanx Satura* (Genoa, 1963), pp. 267–82.

11. As Faral has noted in *Arts poétiques,* p. 116, Matthew's terminology is not based upon Horace. The terms come from the *Ad Herennium,* VI, 10, 15 and IV, 11, 16.

12. This line is an imitation of Horace, *Art of Poetry,* 152.

13. Horace is speaking of dramatic poetry. Matthew has obviously read Horace carefully but seems unaware that fully one-third of the *Art of Poetry* concerns drama.

14. Matthew derives Caesar's name from *caesus,* the past participle of *caedere:* "to cut, to slay." This etymology, which is found in Isidore (*Etymol.,* IX, 3, 12), is based upon the fact the Caesar was surgically delivered; cf. our term "cesarean section."

15. This portrait is bracketed as an interpolation by Faral, who writes, "Ce portrait est certainement une interpolation, ainsi qu'il results du § 58 ci-dessous" [the portrait of Beroe] (*Arts poétiques,* p. 127). Matthew does, however, quote the closing lines in II, 33.

16. Of this line Sedgwick says, "Cf. Henricus Septimell., *Div. Fort.* iv, 156: Fac amet Hypolitus mente Priapus erit" ("Notes," p. 333). The Latin reads, "Let Hippolytus fall in love, then he will be Priapus."

17. Matthew writes threefold. I have followed the sense of this passage in the translation.

18. This verse is discussed by Paul Lehmann, *Die Parodie im Mittelalter,* 2nd ed. (Stuttgart, 1963), pp. 51–53.

19. Matthew does not accurately quote Lucan who wrote, "Sullanam solito tibi lambere ferrum." Matthew's quotation reads, "Solitus Sillanum lambere ferrum." The inaccuracy does not affect Matthew's use of the line.

20. Matthew errs; the source is Juvenal, *Satires,* VII, 145.

21. Matthew errs; the source is Virgil, *Aeneid,* V, 230.

22. I doubt that Matthew is referring to any one passage in the orations against Verres. There is no extended passage setting forth the beauties of Sicily in the Verrine Orations.

23. There is a break in the sense here; see Faral, *Arts poétiques,* p. 148, n. 1. I have tried to give a coherent rendition of the text before me.

24. Matthew gives *occide,* the imperative of *occido* (kill). The standard medieval version of the cry of the nightingale was "Oci! Oci!" This cry may have been onomatopoetic. Matthew seems to have interpreted "Oci" as the imperative of the Old French *occir* (kill). See Raby, *Secular Latin Poetry,* II, 31, n. 55 and *Christian Latin Poetry,* p. 426, n. 3. Matthew may have been influenced by Ovid, *Metamorphoses,* VI, 669: "Neque enim de pectore caedis excessere notae." *Caedis* may have suggested *occide.* See Faral, *Arts poétiques,* p. 148, n. a.

25. Cf. Ovid, *Metamorphoses,* VI, 673. Tereus is the hoopoe.

26. The virgin is Nature, the virgin goddess. The text of the final couplet is

    Praedicti sibi fontis aquam, sibi floris amicat
    Blanditias, genii virgo, studentis opus.

Sedgwick glosses the last line: "a maid, the masterpiece of laboring Nature" ("Notes," p. 334). This reading hardly fits the context. My reading is supported by Winthrop Wetherbee, who calls the final couplet "almost perversely obscure" (*Platonism and Poetry,* p. 150)

27. Boethius, *Consolation of Philosophy,* I, Prose, 1, 13.

28. This is a parody of Lucan, *Pharsalia,* I, 92.

29. The medieval grammarians such as Donatus and Priscian considered nouns and adjectives as a single part of speech because both were declined.

Donatus writes, "How many attributes has a noun? Six. What? Quality, comparison, gender, number, form, case. . . . How many degrees of comparison are there? Three. What? Positive, as learned; comparative, as more learned; superlative, as most learned." *The Ars Minor of Donatus,* trans. Wayland J. Chase, Univ. Wisc. Stud. Soc. Sci. Hist. No. 11 (Madison, 1926), p. 29.

30. Horace says perhaps one can draw a cypress, but of what value is that if one is being paid to paint a sailor swimming from a shipwrecked vessel (*Poet.,* 19–21); Matthew seems to understand the quotation as implying an easy task.

31. Cf. Horace, *Satires,* I, 5, 100: "Apella the Jew may believe it, but not I."

32. Cf. Ibid., 7, 3.

33. Matthew is thinking of the use of these words in the pentameter line of an elegiac. See Sedgwick, "Style and Vocabulary," pp. 360–61.

34. Matthew's text reads: "in Cathegoricis Sillogismis: 'Multotiens res teneris auribus accomodatus senior philosophicae tractus eliminat.' " Boethius in *De syllogismo categorico* wrote, "Quandoquidem res teneris auribus accomodatas saepa severior tractatus eliminat" (Migne, *Patrologia Latina,* XLIV, 793 D). The difference in sense is minimal.

35. Matthew writes "trasonitae," a reference to Thraso, the braggart in the *Miles gloriosus* of Plautus. Faral, *Arts poétiques,* p. 166, notes the parallel with Sidonius Apollinaris, *Epistle* I, 9.

36. Leonine verse is hexameter with internal rhyme. It was developed from the cursus (accentual cadence) in the epistolary style of Pope Leo I, hence the name leonine. See Curtius, *European Literature,* p. 151.

37. This is the influence of Donatus who lists seventeen figures; see Keil, *Grammatici Latini,* IV, 397–402. Matthew omits *prolepsis* (anticipation), *syllepsis* (a single word modifying or governing two or more words though it agrees with only one), *homoeoptoton* (use of words with same inflections that rhyme), and *hirmos* (periodic sentence).

38. The someone is Peter Riga in whose *Aurora* this couplet occurs with quite a different reference. See *Aurora Petri Regiae Biblia Versificatata,* ed. Paul Beichner (Notre Dame, Ind., 1965), I, xxxix and lines 573–74, p. 364.

39. Matthew's quotation reads, "Quique lacus liquidae latus quisque aspera dumis." Faral, *Arts poétiques,* p. 170, notes that the correct text from Virgil is "Quaeque lacus late liquidos, quaequae aspera dumis."

40. I have substituted a verse of my own to illustrate the figures discussed by Matthew; his text reads,

> Eligo, flecto, peto, confirmo, mulceo, servo,
> Vota, datis, stuprum, foedus, amore, fidem.

41. I do not find this statement in the standard modern edition of Isidore. The line from Ennius is quoted once (*Etym.,* I, 26, 14) where Isidore commends Virgil for not using the figure throughout the entire line: "Sid bene hoc temperat Virgilius, dum non toto versu utitur hanc figuram, ut Ennius, sed nunc in principio versus tantum."

42. Donatus says there are thirteen tropes (Keil, *Grammatici Latini,* IV, 399). Matthew omits *catachresis* (improper or unnatural use of a word), *antonomasia* (use of an epithet instead of a proper name), *hyperbaton* (transposition of words to an unnatural order), *hyperbole* and *homoeosis* (resemblance).

43. Mattew errs; the source is Isidore, *Etymologies,* I, 37, 3.

44. Matthew writes, "Floridor prato niveo, etc." As Faral notes (*Arts poétiques,* p. 173), Ovid's text reads, "Candidor nivei folio, Galatea, ligustri, Floridor pratis": O Galatea, whiter than the snow-leafed privet, Flowerier than the meadows.

45. In listing antithesis as a trope, Matthew departs from his sources and from the customary treatment of figures and tropes. Isidore lists antithesis as a figure (*Etym.,* I, 36, 21); Donatus does not treat it as either. See n. 14 in the Introduction.

46. Matthew seems to be referring to his topological description in I, 111. There is obviously a lacuna in the text, since these lines do not appear there.

47. Donatus says that there are seven types of allegory (Keil, *Grammatici Latini,* IV, 401). In addition to *enigma* there are irony, *antiphrasis* (irony in a single word), *charientismos* (euphemism), *paroemia* (use of proverb apt for the circumstances), sarcasm, and *asteismos* (urbane expression).

48. This is found in Symphosius, the *Aenigmata* of Tully, Aldhelm, and Tatwine; see Manitius, *Geschichte,* III, 742.

49. He is probably referring to Marbod of Rennes; see note 17 in the Introduction.

50. H. R. Fairclough glosses the phrase as "a rendering of the Greek proverb . . . which orginally referred to the great expense of a self-indulgent life at Corinth. Here, however, the application is very different, viz., that not everyone can gain the prize of virtue." Horace, *Satires, Epistles, Ars Poetica,* Loeb Classical Library (Cambridge, Mass., and London, 1966), p. 363, n. d. It is obvious that Matthew gives the proverb yet another application.

51. These terms are defined in the Appendix.

52. Wetherbee points out that "Matthew's view of creativity involves the same tripartite conception of mental activity employed by Guillaume [William of Conches] and Bernardus [Silvestris]" (*Platonism and Poetry,* p. 146, n. 43).

53. In the passage from Virgil, *pars* (some) is feminine; *arduus* (erect) and *pulverulentus* (stirring up dust) are both masculine although they modify *pars.* In the passage from Statius, *haec manus* (this troop) is feminine singular; *secuti* (following) is masculine plural.

54. In the passage from Virgil, Matthew is objecting to *Ardebat; ardeo* (burn or glow) is not a transitive verb. In the passage from Statius, he is objecting to the use of *anhelat; anhelo* with an accusative (*proelia*) means pant for or desire.

55. A stock example from Donatus, *Ars grammatica,* in Keil, *Grammatici Latini,* IV, 395; the line may be a parody of Ennius by Lucilius as suggested by Curtius, *European Literature,* p. 493, n. 8. See Willy Morel, *Fragmenta poetarum latinorum* (Leipzig, 1927), p. 172. It also occurs in a slightly different form in Alexander of Villedieu's *Doctrinale* (Monumenta germaniae paedagogica, xii, 1893), verse 2396.

56. I am unable to find this quotation in Lucan.

57. Matthew errs; the source is Virgil, *Aeneid,* X, 180.

58. Max Manitius says that this verse was known from Papias: "Ausserdem der aus Papias bekannte Vers 4, 12 p. 183 [in Faral] *Cresus perdet Alim transgressus plurima regna,"* *Geschichte,* III, 742.

59. Matthew's objection here is obscure. Faral (*Arts poétiques,* p. 183) prints Matthew's text as "Arrige(s) aures, (o) Pamphyle"; John Sargeaunt, *Terence,* Loeb Classical Library (Cambridge, Mass., and London, 1912), I, 102, gives the text as "Arrige auris, Pamphile." *Arrige* (perk up) is an imperative

and makes better sense than the second person singular *arriges*. Sedgwick ("Notes," p. 336) glosses the passage thus: "*cacephaton:* apparently ΚαΚε+ φατου *'obscura pronuntiatio.'* The illustration is thus explained by Eugraphius because *arrigere aures* (1.5) is properly used of a beast; cf. D. Reichling's note on Alexander of Villedieu's *Doctrinale* (Mon. Germ. Paedagog., xii, 1893), v. 2380.' This hardly applies to blurred pronunciation. Virgil uses *arrigere aures* to refer to Anchises in *Aeneid*, II, 303.

60. *Tapinosis* is the use of a term that debases the subject under discussion, namely, "the president politicked on his visit." *Cacosyntheton* is the use of words in other than the normal order. *Eclipsis* is ellipsis.

61. The *Barbarismus* (*Ars maior,* III) of Donatus was a popular grammatical text in the Middle Ages. It is in Keil, *Grammatici Latini,* IV, 393–402.

62. For a discussion of the *gradus amoris* see Lionel Friedman, "Gradus Amoris," *Romance Philology,* XIX (1965), 165–77; Matthew's divergence from the general tradition is discussed on pp. 170–72.

63. Matthew writes "Garamantes," an African tribe; in the Middle Ages they suggested a backward people.

64. Matthew writes, "teste Boecio, contraria contrariis conveniunt." I do not find the phrase in Boethius's *Consolation* or in Lane Cooper's *Concordance to Boethius* (Cambridge, Mass., 1928).

65. See note 21 in the Introduction.

66. Matthew gives the title of Horace's book as "Sermonum," which Faral glosses: "Erreur. Lire: Satirarum" (*Arts poétiques,* p. 190, n. 1). There is no error. *Sermones* (Conversations), not *Saturae,* was the title given the work by Horace (See *Ep.,* I, 4, 1 and II, 2, 60). This title was common in Matthew's time. My translation follows modern nomenclature.

67. Arnulf of Orléans, as he is generally known today, was a rival scholar. See n. 30 in the Introduction.

68. Cf. Acts 9:5; 26:14.

69. Matthew conflates Prov. 26:4 and 26:5.

70. This is found in Symphosius, the *Aenigmata* of Tully, Aldhelm, and Tatwine; see Manitius, *Geschichte* III, 742.

71. Cf. Virgil, *Eclogues,* VII, 26.

72. A parody of Ovid, *Tristia,* IV, 10, 26.

73. The law of Otho (67 B.C.) provided that the knights, the wealthy middle class, occupy the first fourteen rows of the theater behind the orchestra where the senators sat. Authored by the knight Otho, it suggests vanity. Cf. Juvenal., *Satires,* III, 159: "Such is the will of vain Otho who makes distinctions between us." "The well of a sot" (*putealque bibonis*) is a word play on a line from Horace: "Forum putealque Libonis mandabo siccis": To the sober I assign a life of business and commerce. The puteal of Libo was a place in Rome where financial affairs were transacted.

I N D E X